The **CSS** **Pocket**Guide

Chris **Casciano**

Ginormous knowledge, pocket-sized.

The CSS Pocket Guide

Chris Casciano

Peachpit Press
1249 Eighth Street
Berkeley, CA 94710
510/524-2178
510/524-2221 (fax)

Find us on the Web at: www.peachpit.com
To report errors, please send a note to: errata@peachpit.com

Peachpit Press is a division of Pearson Education.

Editor: Kim Wimpsett
Technical editors: Michael Bester and Kimberly Blessing
Production Editor: Myrna Vladic
Compositor: David Van Ness
Indexer: Ann Rogers
Cover Design: Peachpit Press
Interior Design: Peachpit Press

ISBN-13: 978-0-321-73227-9
ISBN-10: 0-321-73227-8

9 8 7 6 5 4 3 2 1

Printed and bound in the United States of America

About the Author

Chris Casciano started building web sites professionally in 1997 when web development meant working with tables and font tags, sticking to a "web-safe" color palette, and worrying about load times for those using dial-up modems. He is now working as freelance web developer, spending the last nine years in the trenches architecting and building web sites for digital agencies and their clients. Throughout his career Chris has explored ways to implement emerging technologies such as HTML5, CSS3, and JavaScript in practical ways—balancing the bleeding edge with the responsibilities of serving a diverse audience. His personal projects and writing have inspired industry leaders with projects such as Daily CSS Fun in 2002 serving as inspiration for the popular CSS Zen Garden. Since 2003, Chris has been an advocate for adoption of web standards as a member of the Web Standards Project.

His personal web site, Place Name Here (*http://placenamehere.com*), which is now home to a blog covering both web development and his other passion of digital photography, has been online since 1998.

Acknowledgments

I have to thank Clifford Colby, Bruce Hyslop, and Lenny Burdette for the opportunity to write this book and their encouragement along the way.

I must also thank my editors. Kim Wimpsett at Peachpit Press deserves credit for all her hard work including her endless battles like those with square brackets and the words *then/than*. My friends and technical editors Michael Bester and Kimberly Blessing were invaluable in helping craft the pages of this book and kept me in line and on topic.

Thanks to my family, including Mom, Dad, Mari and Justin, Joanna and Jared (and Lily), and Matt, for everything.

Finally, thanks to the people I've shared the Internet with over the past 15 years—whether through online communities from webdesign-l to b3s or my co-workers and those in the NYC tech community. You shaped my understanding of our industry and the technologies we use, and you encouraged me to keep on keepin' on throughout my career and my life.

Contents

Introduction

The styling of web documents has evolved a great deal from the early days of the Web when font tags, tables, and HTML attributes scattered everywhere were just what you had to do to make pages look good (or get that animated GIF of a flame repeating across your whole page).

The CSS Pocket Guide will teach you the building blocks of styling documents with CSS, give you an arsenal of modern development techniques, and help you navigate the ever-changing landscape of web browsers and specifications, including CSS3.

Who Should Read This Book

Anyone designing or building web pages should understand CSS. This book offers an overview of CSS and the building blocks of the language to get you going and is geared toward novice and intermediate developers.

Before reading this book, it is important to have some exposure to and understand how to read and write HTML—the markup and content that the CSS code in this book is used to style.

What You Will Learn

This book covers CSS including CSS 2.1 and parts of CSS3.

- The beginning of the book covers the building blocks of CSS and how to use those tools to create layouts with CSS.
- The book then goes on to discuss how to use CSS to style the content elements that are often placed into the parts of the layout grid you've just learned to build.
- The last part of the book dives deeper into specific topics such as working with different types of media or creating form layouts.

Along the way, there is also discussion of current best practices in web development and information on upcoming changes to CSS included in CSS3 and beyond.

What You Won't Find in This Book

It is impossible to cover CSS in all its applications and in all the different ways it can be encountered in one book written by one person. Although the language is covered in detail and this book can serve as a great reference for those learning other aspects of web design and development, it does not attempt to cover any of the following in detail:

- It does not attempt to teach you what HTML is or how to write good HTML.
- It does not attempt to teach you anything about JavaScript or scripting things such as animations or Ajax. But it will make a useful reference for the CSS properties you will often manipulate with JavaScript.
- It does not attempt to teach principles of good visual or interactive design. It will, however, give you the tools to implement those designs.
- It also it does not explicitly cover CSS as applied to documents other than HTML (such as SVG).

What You Need to Follow Along

All you need is a text editor to write CSS code or review the example CSS and HTML code, ideally one with syntax highlighting such as Notepad2 for Windows or TextWrangler for Mac OS X (both are free). You'll also need a web browser to view the results of any code you write. A visual, or WYSIWYG, editor such as Dreamweaver can also be used, provided it offers a "code" or "source" view.

The figures used to demonstrated CSS code throughout this button were all generated with actual CSS code. These full code examples, including the HTML5 documents, can be downloaded from *http://www.peachpit.com/csspocketguide* so you can follow along, review the examples in different browsers, or edit the examples and experiment with them.

Resources

It goes without saying that a topic at the core of web development will have a large number of great resources on the Web.

- Check out the W3C's CSS Working Groups Current Work index of the CSS specifications. *http://www.w3.org/Style/CSS/current-work*
- You can also refer to the detailed browser support charts and other web development articles by Peter-Paul Koch at QuirksMode.org. *http://quirksmode.org/*
- The WaSP InterAct Curriculum project offers a full and ongoing curriculum for learning and teaching web development and web design including CSS. *http://interact.webstandards.org/*
- The Mozilla Developer Center offers a complete reference of the CSS language and is great for looking things up in a flash. *https://developer.mozilla.org/en/CSS_Reference*
- The Opera Developer Network offers articles, tutorials, and references for all areas of web development, including a curriculum you can walk through and teach yourself. *http://dev.opera.com/*

Writing CSS

Unlike a programming language such as JavaScript, there isn't that much to the syntax of CSS and the makeup of CSS rules. But the following sections highlight some things you should know before jumping into the complexities of what the simple syntax can do.

Case Sensitivity

CSS is case insensitive. For example, the `color` property is equivalent to the `COLOR` property, and a `px` unit is the same as a `PX` or `Px` unit. By convention, properties and values are typically written using lowercase characters, and that is the convention followed in this book.

Parts of the code not under the control of CSS such as file paths to style sheet documents, images, element names, classes, and IDs *may* be case sensitive and are defined at their source. For example, the file path on one server may be case sensitive, but on another server or your local machine it may not be. For markup, elements in HTML documents are case insensitive; however, elements in XML-based documents are.

To avoid confusion or code bugs, it is best to match the case in your code regardless of whether it will be enforced.

Comments

There is only one way to write a comment in CSS—beginning with the two characters /* and ending with the same two characters reversed, */. Any text, code, or whitespace between those two is ignored.

```
/* this is a comment */
```

Whitespace

In CSS, whitespace—including space characters, tabs, and line breaks—has no meaning outside of its use as a descendent selector (Chapter 3) or as a separator for multiple values in a single declaration. Outside of those two cases, it is considered optional. It is up to you to use whitespace (or not) to format your CSS to help with the organization and readability of your code.

Quoting and Escaping Quotes

The single quote (') and double quote (") can be used interchangeably to wrap string values in CSS (though if a string starts with one, it must end with the same one).

The backslash (\) is the escape character in CSS. It can be used to escape a quote mark that is part of a string (or another backslash that should appear as part of the string). The backslash character can also be used to include characters via their character codes.

For some string-like references, such as with a `url()` reference, it is also allowable to leave off the quote marks around a string.

Keywords, such as color names, are not strings and must not be quoted.

Tools

Building web pages while wrangling browser bugs takes more than just a text editor and a browser. The following are a few categories of tools that are invaluable additions to your toolbox.

Validation Tools

Validation tools parse your HTML or CSS documents checking for conformance with the designated specification in areas such as syntax errors, missing or improperly nested HTML tags, unknown CSS properties, illegal values, or other coding problems. The W3C validation service (*http://jigsaw.w3.org/css-validator/*) is one commonly used validator.

As a tool, the errors a validation service can uncover may help identify where visual bugs you're seeing in browsers could derive from. For example, it is common that a missing closing tag may cause styles to bleed out of the area you would have expected. But be careful and understand validation errors before reacting to them because some code that you want to use, such as vendor extensions for experimental CSS3 implementations, may also be reported as an error based on the validator's settings.

Web Inspectors

Web inspectors (or DOM inspectors) are tools that allow you to view the document tree, CSS properties, and other information about a web page as it appears in your browser, often with a click on the element itself. These tools are invaluable when writing and debugging CSS code, providing real-time information about style properties and pointing out which style rules contributed to the element's appearance.

- *Internet Explorer*: Starting with version 8, Internet Explorer includes Developer Tools, a set of built-in tools including the ability to inspect HTML elements and view CSS information. To launch the tools, press F12 or select Tools > Developer Tools from the menu in IE. For older versions of IE, including 6 and 7, Microsoft offers a downloadable extension called the Internet Explorer Developer Toolbar.
- *Firefox*: Among its other features, the Firebug extension for Firefox (*http://www.getfirebug.org/*) allows for viewing and editing of the document tree and style property cascade. Once installed, you can open Firebug directly or by right-clicking an element in the page and choosing Inspect Element.
- *Safari*: Safari on OS X and Windows comes with a built-in set of developer tools including a web inspector. These tools are disabled by default, but you can enable them from the Advanced panel inside Safari's preferences. Once enabled, you can open it from the Develop menu or by right-clicking an element in the page and choosing Inspect Element.
- *Chrome*: Chrome also ships with built-in developer tools with similar features to those already mentioned. To access the tools, select View > Development > Developer Tools from the menu or right-click an element in the page and choose Inspect Element.
- *Opera*: Opera Dragonfly is another suite of tools for working with web documents including viewing styling information. To activate Dragonfly, select Tools > Advanced > Opera Dragonfly from the menu in Opera, or right-click an element in the page and choose Inspect Element.

Web Developer Toolbar

Chris Pederick created the Web Developer Toolbar extension (*http://chrispederick.com/work/web-developer/*) for Firefox and Chrome that provides some nifty features not found in standard web inspectors such as the ability to add an overlay above the document that displays the document structure or element attributes, resize your browser window to certain dimensions for testing, or submit the document directly to validation services.

(I take some pride in this tool as it is based on the toolbar I had written for the now long defunct Mozilla Suite, the browser that predated Firefox. That said, Chris deserves all the credit now because he has taken it further and supported it with much more time and energy than I had.)

Yahoo! YSlow and Google Page Speed

Yahoo! YSlow (*http://developer.yahoo.com/yslow/*) is a Firefox add-on geared toward analyzing and improving the performance of web sites in areas such as caching, download sizes, and speeds, as well as reducing the number of requests made to the server delivering the content and all its types of assets.

Through YSlow and its companion suite of tool, you can learn about tools to compress CSS documents; optimize server calls for CSS files, JavaScript files, and images; and perform lots of other performance tricks not covered directly in this book.

Google Page Speed (*http://code.google.com/speed/page-speed/*) is another Firebug add-on in a similar vein as YSlow. It can identify which CSS declarations are not being utilized by an HTML document and it can point out which of your CSS selectors are written inefficiently and why.

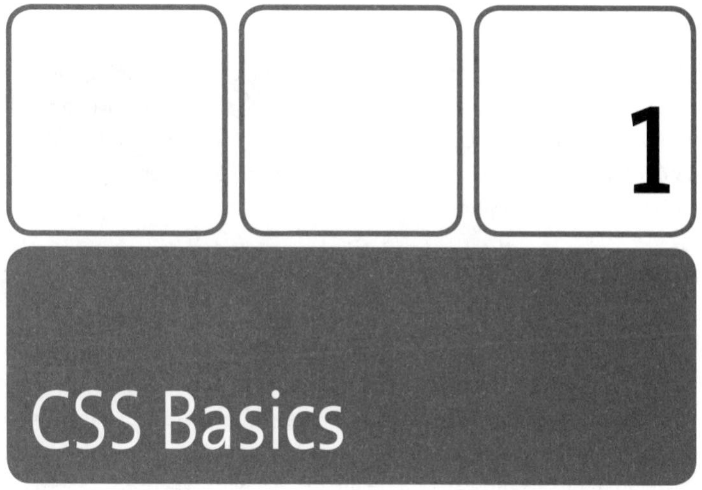

1 CSS Basics

There exists a trinity of standards-based web development technologies that when used in concert can create exciting, vibrant, interactive web sites out of what on their own are just a bunch of text files.

HTML provides the content and structure of the web page, JavaScript supplies the interaction and document manipulation, and CSS provides the presentation and flair.

What Is CSS?

CSS, short for Cascading Style Sheets, is a language for describing the presentational properties of content elements in structured documents such as HTML documents. Though this book will focus on styling HTML content, you can also use CSS for other structured documents such as those created with XML or SVG.

What Are Styles Sheets?

Style sheets provide a set of guidelines for styling a structured document by defining rules for the appearance of different types of content or different contexts that content can be found in. You may have already encountered forms of style sheets or themes in typical office suites or e-mail programs. It is common in presentation software such as PowerPoint or Keynote to pick a theme to start with, where each slide is automatically formatted with the same font sizes, colors, and layouts, rather than starting with a blank slate and designing each slide individually and hoping for them to be consistent when you're done.

As a browser or other user agent loads the HTML content for the document, it also loads the style sheet information. From this style sheet information, it then builds up the set of presentation rules for each individual content item based on its element type, its state, and its location in the document. It will ultimately render each element consistently based on this accumulated set of rules.

Anatomy of a Statement

CSS-based style sheets consist of a list of statements. There are two types of statements: rule sets (referred to as *rules*) and at-rules.

Rule Sets

A *rule set* consists of a selector followed by a declaration block containing declarations of style properties and their values, as explained in the following list (see also **Figure 1.1**).

Figure 1.1
The parts of a rule set.

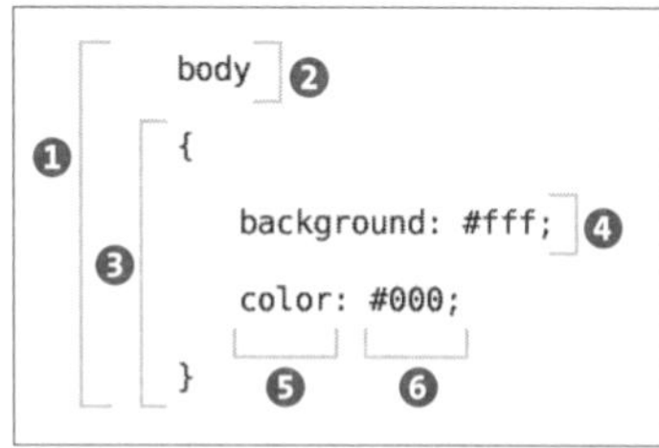

1. *Rule set*: This is the entire definition of a CSS rule, including selector and declaration block, containing individual declarations.
2. *Selector*: The selector includes everything up to the opening curly brace. The selector describes the markup elements to which the contents of declaration block apply. Individual selectors may share a declaration block, with each selector separated with a comma (,).
3. *Declaration block*: The declaration block starts with the left curly brace and ends with the right curly brace. Inside the block there are zero or more declarations, each separated by a semicolon (;).
3. *Declaration*: Each declaration is a colon-separated property-value pair.
5. *Property*: The property is the CSS property that the declaration is targeting.
6. *Value*: This is the value that will be applied to the declared property. The syntax of the value depends on the property but can be things such as keywords, a `<length>`, a `<percentage>`, or a mix of multiple, space-separated types.

Defining Values for Four-Sided Properties

Properties such as `margin`, `padding`, and `border-width` are used to define values for all four sides of a block (whereas `margin-right` defines the right margin alone). These properties, and those like them, can take from one to four space-separated values that are applied to the sides in the following manner:

- If one value is listed (for example, `10px`), that value is applied to all four sides.
- If two values are listed (for example, `10px 5%`), the first value is applied to the top and bottom, while the second is applied to the right and left sides.
- If three values are listed (for example, `10px 5% 20px`), the first value is applied to the top, the second to both the right and left sides, and the last to the bottom.
- If four values are listed (for example, `10px 5% 20px auto`), the values are applied clockwise starting from the top (top, right, bottom, left).

At-Rules

At-rules are statements that begin with the character for at (@), followed by a rule type or identifier, and end with a semicolon. Unlike rule sets, at-rules do not contain declarations directly but offer additional context or commands for the processing of style sheet information. Here's an example:

```
/* include file additional.css */
@import "additional.css"
/* target specific media with contained rules */
```

```
@media print {
    [...]
}
```

Cascading

The *cascading* in CSS is the process that is followed in order to determine which declaration for a given property is applied to a given element in the document. As you'll soon learn, properties—`color`, for instance—can be defined and redefined multiple times, so the browser must determine which of those definitions to apply. The criteria for sorting through the style sheets to determine which property declaration to use is threefold: weight, specificity, and order of appearance.

The *weight* of the declaration is determined by the origin of the style rule. Style rules can be found in one of three sources in descending order of weight:

- *Author style sheets*: These are the style sheets defined along with the source HTML document by the author of the page visited.
- *User style sheets*: User style sheets are CSS documents or other styling preferences selected by the user of the browser.
- *User agent style sheets*: Each user agent applies a default set of presentation rules representing common behaviors for each HTML element (links are highlighted, headings are larger, and so on).

You can learn more about the sources of styling rules in Chapter 2.

The *specificity* of the declaration is determined by how precise the selector used for the element is. A selector that states "any paragraph element" (<p>) is less specific than a selector looking for "any paragraph that occurs inside of a block quote" (`<blockquote><p>`).

note **Specificity is covered in detail in Chapter 3.**

The *order of appearance*, or source order, of the declaration is determined by the order the rules are encountered in the set of documents in a given source category where the later declaration replaces all earlier declarations.

To calculate the winning declaration for a given property, first weight is considered. If multiple declarations share the highest weight source, then specificity is considered. Finally, if multiple declarations share the same, greatest specificity, then order of appearance is used to pick the appropriate declaration to apply.

Figure 1.2 shows the cascade of rules for a link in the footer of the Apple.com home page as viewed in the Safari Web Inspector. Declarations that appear crossed out have been trumped by other declarations of that property higher in the cascading order.

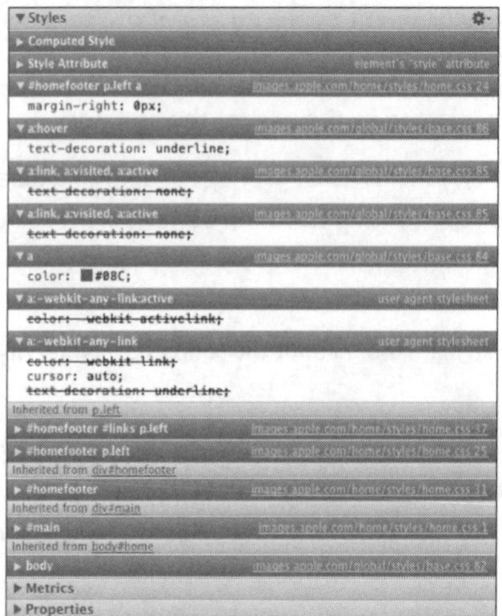

Figure 1.2 *The Safari Web Inspector displaying the cascade.*

Inheritance

The values for some properties, such as `color` and `font-family`, are inherited by child elements of the element where the property was set. If that property was not explicitly declared for the child element, it will use the inherited value for display. In the case of `color`, if the `<body>` element has been set to `black`, then paragraphs, list contents, block quotes, and other children will also have a `color` value of `black`. Because links have a different color defined in the user agent style sheet, they will not appear as black but as the default blue color (or other set default link color).

Inherited values are passed along to child elements as their *computed* value. For example, `font-size` is inherited; thus, the value passed to the child elements would be the final, calculated value in pixels and not the original units, which may have been ems, ens, points, or pixels. If the inherited value were to be in ems instead, the size would then be recalculated for each child that inherited it.

```
<p style="font-size: 10px">
<strong style="2em">
<span>Text</span>
</strong>
</p>
```

In the previous code example, the `font-size` for the `<strong>` element is calculated to be `20px`, and this is the value inherited by the `<span>` element. If the specified value of `2em` was inherited and the size recalculated, the `<span>` would have a font-sized value of `40px` instead. I'll further explain computed values in the next section.

Other properties, such as `width`, `height`, and `margin`, are not inherited and cannot be inherited. This means that although you may place a height value on a `<div>` or `<article>` element of `400px`, all of that `<div>` or `<article>`'s children will continue to use the default value of `height` (`auto`) unless their `height` is explicitly set.

The CSS specification for each property lists whether that property can inherit and whether it will inherit its parent's value by default.

The Importance of Good HTML Roots

A foundation of strong structural and semantic markup is crucial to making designing with CSS easy, readable, and maintainable. Although every individual node in the document tree can be styled explicitly, with the behavior of the cascade, specificity, and inheritance, CSS was designed to take advantage of element context and markup patterns. Poorly crafted markup doesn't provide the contextual clues or "hooks" for styling that good markup practices like the appropriate use of `<div>` or `<section>` elements, a varied level of headings, and using paragraphs rather than line breaks do.

Specified, Computed, Used, and Actual Values

Values come in four flavors depending on where and how they are being referenced. You've already encountered computed values and specified values: the third is the actual value.

- *Specified values*: These are the values as they were coded in the CSS rules.
- *Computed values*: These are the values for a property as they are calculated after applying the cascade and inheritance but before the document is processed or rendered. Units like ems are calculated and turned into fixed values (pixels for most devices), paths to files are made absolute, and inherited values are inherited.
- *Used values*: After all the values are calculated and the document is processed, the value of some other properties such as percentage or `auto`-based widths that rely on the dimensions of a parent element

to be known are calculated into their fixed-width equivalents. When these calculations are complete and the page is rendered, the resulting values are the used values. Though the naming is unfortunate, it is these used values that are encountered when scripting CSS through the `getComputedStyle` DOM API or viewing the computed tab in Firebug.

- *Actual values*: After all the calculations are done and a browser has processed the document, there are some occasions where the used value cannot be rendered, so the browser must approximate the used value, creating the actual value. This can occur when a fractional pixel unit results from a calculation (50 percent of 99 pixels) or when a low-color-depth, monochrome display isn't capable of rendering the exact color calculated.

Block, Inline, and Replaced Elements

There are three main types of element types in HTML documents (a broad generalization) whose intended content types dictate their behavior in CSS and presentation. There are elements that serve as containers for other content (`<div>`, `<p>`), there are elements that differentiate types of text content (`<a>`, `<strong>`), and there are elements that refer to external content (`<img>`, `<object>`).

Throughout this book the first type are *block elements*, the second type *inline elements*, and the last inline *replaced elements*.

Web Standards and Specifications

The World Wide Web Consortium (W3C) along with other standards bodies such as WHATWG and IETF produce standards and specification documents for everything from CSS to the HTTP protocol that computers on the Internet use to communicate. You can find the specifications for CSS and HTML on the W3C web site at *http://www.w3.org/*.

CSS2, CSS2.1, CSS3, Drafts, Recommendations, Ack!

We're at a moment in time where the state of the CSS "standard," while active and exciting, can often be confusing. The W3C's CSS Working Group consists of representatives from browser vendors and other technical experts who are actively writing and maintaining the specifications. At first look, there are a lot of specification documents, and they're all at different points in the process.

There are many states a specification moves through on its way to being finalized, gathering comments and test implementations along the way:

- *Working Draft*: A Working Draft (WD) is the earliest definition of the specification. The document itself will often be loaded with notes, questions, or incomplete references. Working Drafts are useful to see what is ahead and for browser vendors to create test implementations. There will be certainly be changes to the document and possibly to individual property definitions in the future because no consensus on the content of the document has yet been reached.
- *Last Call Working Draft*: When issues, conflicts, and questions in the Working Draft are resolved, there is a Last Call (LC) comment period announced to solicit feedback on the draft.
- *Candidate Recommendation*: After that Last Call period, a draft may move onto a Candidate Recommendation (CR), and the working group solicits test implementations from vendors to make sure what has been proposed is workable.
- *Proposed Recommendation*: To be a Proposed Recommendation (PR), the specification is stable, and vendors have created interoperable implementations.
- *Recommendation*: The bill has become a law—or a finalized Recommendation (R) as it were.

The process to make it to a Recommendation can be quite drawn out. Although CSS3 is big on everyone's mind, CSS 2.1 is just now ready to become a Proposed Recommendation, so it is sometimes hard to nail down by specification alone what is ready for you to spend time to learn or to use on a site.

Here is where the various specifications are along that line and that you can start using today:

- *CSS2*: CSS2 became a Recommendation in 1998. As a specification, it has been superseded by CSS2.1, though the term "CSS2" may be used to refer to either.
- *CSS2.1*: As this book is being written in the later part of 2010, the CSS2.1 specification is being readied for PR status. CSS2.1 made changes to CSS2 by updating technical descriptions and removing properties to better reflect implementation (or total lack of implementation) of the previous Recommendation.
- *CSS3*: With CSS3, the specification has been split into modules as a way to control the complexity of any given piece of the large undertaking as well as provide user agents a clear means to carve out which areas they may not support due to technical device limitations. Some modules are CRs with better support and implementations, and others have yet to be written.

For the updated status of CSS2.1 and the various CSS3 modules, see *http://www.w3.org/Style/CSS/current-work*. And with all these specifications, CSS3 modules in particular, refer not just to the specification status but also to browser compatibility charts for implementation details on the various properties you may want to use.

HTML 4, XHTML, and HTML5

Which HTML specification (or draft specification) you choose to write markup based on is entirely up to you (or your supervisors or clients). Though HTML5 may offer some exciting new features such as additional structural elements and web form components, they all are "standards" and work equally well with CSS.

It is important, however, that you do pick and write to both the DOCTYPE and codification of the standards and the semantic rules of the specification. Though there are rules for handling markup errors in some specifications, invalid markup such as improperly nested elements or tags that are never closed can often lead to unexpected styling consequences. In a similar vein, poor markup semantics may muddy up your selectors and make your CSS code difficult to follow.

User Agents, Browsers, and Devices

The most common piece of software that consumes and renders the display of web pages and CSS is the web browser.

The term for the broad category of anything that can consume a web document is a *user agent*. User agents include the typical web browser but also tools such as screen-reading applications, feed readers, Google and other search engine spiders, and other programmatic interfaces.

Devices are the hardware the user agents run on and often dictate what features that user agent can support. A smartphone may have a smaller screen than a desktop computer, a printer takes on the characteristics of a printed page, and a Wii may display content on a standard-definition television screen.

User agents on devices such as desktop browsers where the content is displayed on one large canvas (or viewport) are classified as *continuous media*, while printers, which output onto multiple fixed-sized parts, are considered *paged media*.

Through most of this book you'll be learning about CSS as it applies to web browsers and continuous media on screen-based devices, with a notable break in Chapter 12.

Working with CSS

Now that you know everything you ever wanted to know about the definition of CSS and the specification process, you might need to know how you get actual CSS code into your web pages and what CSS really looks like.

Attaching Styles to HTML

Before you start writing CSS, you have to know where to put the code. There are a few ways to define rules for your content, some based on external files that can be shared between multiple HTML documents on a site and some that are more specific to a page or even individual elements.

HTML `<link>` *element*

You can use the HTML `<link>` element in the <head> of a document to specify an external CSS document. This document does not contain markup or script elements, only CSS code (rules and comments).

```
<head>
<link rel="stylesheet" type="text/css" src="global.css">
</head>
```

The `type` attribute defines which language is used in the style sheet. It is required for HTML4 and XHTML, but it is optional in HTML5 (defaulting to `text/css`). The `src` attribute defines the location of the CSS document; if it is a relative path, it is relative to the location of the referencing HTML document.

HTML `<style>` *element*

You can use the HTML `<style>` element in the `<head>` of a document to wrap CSS code to be applied to the document.

```
<head>
<style type="text/css">
[...]
</style>
</head>
```

The `type` attribute defines which language is used in the style sheet. It is required for HTML4 and XHTML, but it is optional in HTML5 (defaulting to `text/css`).

HTML5 also defines a scope attribute that allows the `<style>` element to be used inside a block of content, not just the head element.

`@import` *Rule*

You can use the `@import` rule at the top of any block of CSS code or CSS document to define another CSS document to be included into the current document or code block. The `@import` rule must precede all other rules in the document (with the exception of the proposed `@charset` rule from CSS3).

```
@import "imported.css"
```

HTML `style` *Attribute*

HTML content elements (those not associated with the document <head>) have a `style` attribute that can be used to assign a semicolon-separated list of CSS declarations to that specific element.

```
<p style="color: pink">A Pink Paragraph</p>
```

This attribute is an unwieldy method of styling an entire document but can occasionally be useful on a project where it is important for style information to be matched with the HTML content such as when sharing HTML content across sites or defining one-off special cases for styling an element.

JavaScript and the DOM

JavaScript can access style sheets and style properties via the Document Object Model (DOM). JavaScript can be used to set styles via the `style` object on an element or to read current styling information (used values) via the `getComputedStyle` method.

You can also use JavaScript to read the contents of style sheets via the `document.styleSheets` object, which is a useful technique for creating bridge libraries to bring support for unsupported CSS properties or selectors to older browsers (discussed in Chapter 13).

note **Multiword CSS properties when accessed though JavaScript are camel cased, rather than hyphenated. In other words, `margin-left` becomes `marginLeft`.**

Coding Styles

CSS does not rely on whitespace or indentation to parse the values, but consistent use of whitespace can make code easier to follow—as can thoughtful organization of the rules in a document and good use of CSS comments. There is no one right way to format and organize CSS code, but this section will provide some place to start as you learn CSS and build and test your code.

Code Locations

CSS has its greatest value when it's shared across multiple documents or entire sites rather than rewritten or copy and pasted from document to document. As a result, it is common to break style rules into groups of how they apply to your content:

- *Global styles*: This includes style information that can be applied to the entire site. These styles should be in one of the first linked external CSS documents.
- *Section or page type styles*: This includes style information that can be applied to a subsection or alternate page type augmenting or changing the global styles. These styles can be in a separate external style sheet linked after the global CSS document only from that type of page, or included in the global CSS document with some `class` or `id` used on an HTML element such as <body> to distinguish the page type.
- *Page or content-specific styles*: This includes style information that is shared among pages infrequently or not at all. If it is a small amount of code, it can be placed in either the global or section CSS documents; however, if more extensive, a third linked document may be used.
- *Unique documents*: It may be that a page type on a site is truly unique or that a document is intended to not be part of a site or set of other documents. This is the case with the code used to generate the figures throughout this book. In these cases, a style block can cut down the number of external files that need managing or requests being made to the server.

The implementation of this type of structure, if all those levels of granularity are helpful, could look something like the following:

```
<head>
[...]
<link type="text/css" href="styles/global.css">
<link type="text/css" href="styles/forums.css">
<link type="text/css" href="styles/forum_help.css">
[...]
</head>
```

Commenting and Code Documentation

Though individual CSS rules are quite easy to read and understand ("this rule makes the body background white"), even the most basic web sites will have a few hundred lines of CSS code. Since CSS has no inherent structure to the code like HTML has its document tree, using CSS comments to distinguish sections and structure of the document as well as to keep notes on individual selectors or properties is important.

Start each document with some information on what the document should contain and an inventory of its contents so it is easy to follow.

```
/**
 * Global Styles
 * yournewwebsite.com
 *
 * Contents:
 * 1. Basic HTML elements
 * 2. Layout Grid
 * 3. Header Content Styles
 * 4. Page Content Styles
 * 4a. Index Page Content
```

(continues on next page)

```
 * 4b. Article Page Content
 * 5. Footer Content Styles
 */
```

To distinguish sections of the document such as marking where the layout grid is specified or where the styles for forms are located, use a one- or two-line comment that catches the eye when you run through the document.

```
/* ******* Footer Content Styles ******* */
```

To comment on a CSS rule, place a comment on the line before the rule.

```
/* make link big and colorful */
div.newsletterSignup a {
   font-size: 2em;
   color: pink;
}
```

To comment on an individual property or value, place a comment after the declaration or on the line before it.

```
article {
   min-width: 500px; /* wide enough for image content */
}
```

Arrangement of Selectors

Comments aren't the only way to help make large amounts of CSS code easier to read, scan, and maintain. Coding conventions for formatting the appearance CSS rules and code organization of those rules are another key aid.

Whitespace surrounding rules and the indentation (or not) of rules and individual declarations should be consistent. There are two main camps in the formatting for rules, and both have their pluses and minuses.

Throughout this book I commonly have written rules with one declaration per line and indented one tab from the left.

```
#footer form.newsletter input[type=text] {
	width: 120px;
	margin-bottom: 5px;
	color: #666;
	background: #ccc;
}
```

This makes it easy to scan and comment on individual declarations but may make it more difficult to scan through groups of selectors as you work on your code. Having an entire rule on one line may make scanning and identifying groups of rules much easier though requires some horizontal scanning to find individual properties or values.

```
#footer { [...] }
#footer form.login { [...] }
#footer form.login input[type=text] { [...] }
#footer form.newsletter { [...] }
#footer form.newsletter p { [...] }
#footer form.newsletter input[type=text] { [...] }
#footer form.newsletter input[type=submit] { [...] }
```

How you organize your rules is also important. The cascade's reliance on appearance order for selectors and specificity is a good starting point for seeing how a document might be organized—with general and generic rules first, followed by more specific rules for unique content types or markup structures. But at some point your selectors will be targeting more unique types of content and not matching the same content elements, so order isn't important. Here it is good to keep code pertaining to the same blocks or types of content together (all login form content together and all footer content together, for example).

The suggested comment for opening a document earlier in this chapter shares a good example of how one might organize the overall structure of a site's global CSS document.

```
/*
 * Contents:
 * 1. Basic HTML elements
 * 2. Layout Grid
 * 3. Header Content Styles
 * 4. Page Content Styles
 * 4a. Index Page Content
 * 4b. Article Page Content
 * 5. Footer Content Styles
 */
```

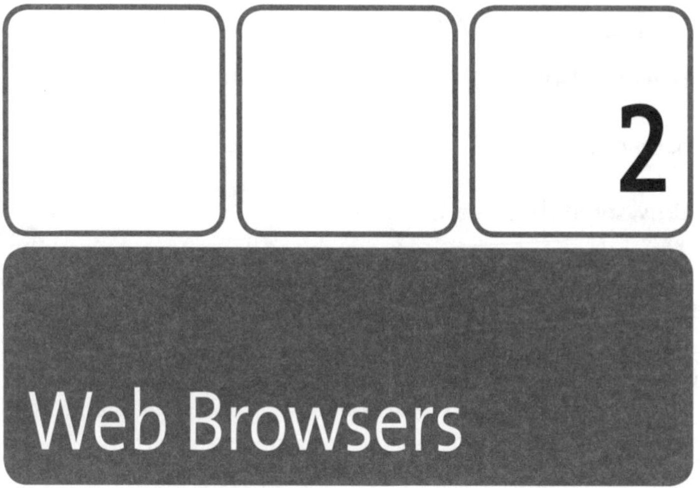

Web browsers and their openness to consume what the world serves up are why we are able to design such rich sites that are easy to update and alter. Browsers are the yin to the web server's yang. But as a content creator, the plethora of browsers can be a drag.

In this chapter, you will see some of the ways web browsers impact your CSS code, learn how to embrace the different platforms and devices that may view the pages you build, and see some frequent browser-related quirks and common ways to deal with them.

Where Do Styles Come From?

Before any document-specific styles are applied to your pages, browsers apply certain styles based on a combination of browser defaults, application preferences, and advanced user customization.

Browser Style Sheets

Every browser ships with a default or base style sheet. From browser to browser, these settings are common—headings are larger than the base font size, links are underlined, lists have bullets, and some space appears between individual paragraphs.

Browser vendors pick the styling based on a mix of accepted practices and what will work best on their specific operating system and device. These base style sheets act as the foundation for displaying all web pages.

Often, as in the case of lists and bullets, you may choose to not write your own CSS and just go with the defaults. Or, you may want to alter just one or two of these properties and let the rest be, such as changing the margin and padding for list items but leaving the bullet style for list items alone.

If you are the curious type, you can find all eight files that make up the default style sheet for Firefox 3 via the internal URL *resource://gre/res/*. Internet Explorer's base style sheet isn't as accessible, but Jon Neil has tried to reverse engineer it, placing the results at *http://www.iecss.com/*. One look at either, and you're sure to be overwhelmed.

You can simply ignore many of these settings, but some such as margins or padding make creating consistent presentations difficult. In Chapter 13, I'll cover using a "reset" to zero out some of these base style rules to provide an even starting point to code against.

User Settings

In addition to a browser's baseline list of styles that it applies to HTML elements, most browsers allow users to customize a few style properties to make reading and interacting with web sites easier (**Figure 2.1**).

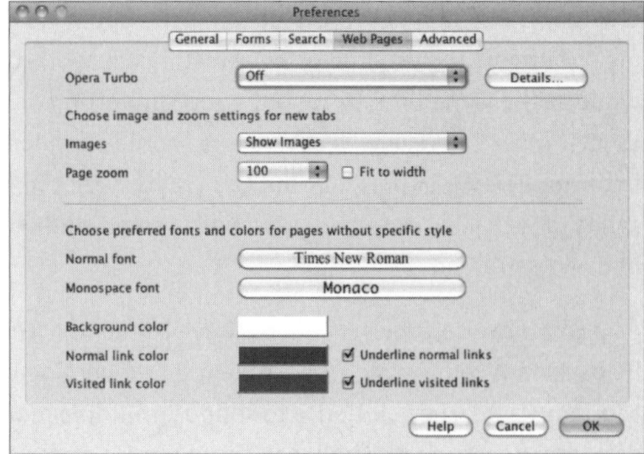

Figure 2.1 *Preferences dialog box in Opera 10.54 for OS X.*

Through a browser's preferences, users can often set whether their browser supports images, the base font size and font family it uses, and the behavior of certain features such as links.

User Style Sheets

Being able to control font sizes and colors is only the beginning. Many browsers offer the ability to go beyond the preference dialog boxes and allow a CSS file to be loaded and applied after the base browser style sheets and before the styles dictated by the Web. This user style sheet can contain any and all of the same rules that you might use to design a web page.

Tools such as the Stylish Firefox extension (*http://userstyles.org/*) provide users who don't know CSS with sample style sheets and an easy way to load them for all sites they visit or to customize specific sites they frequent.

Rendering Modes

The teams building web browsers have the unenviable position of needing to support the way things have historically worked in their browsers while at the same time fixing bugs and supporting new work by the W3C. It may seem like web developers should abandon old and buggy behavior in favor of progress, but the reality is that hundreds of thousands of web sites may have been built, tested, and published with old behaviors in mind.

As a compromise, browser vendors have come up with a way they can be backward compatible while adhering to emerging web standards at the same time. The solution is to support multiple rendering modes and provide a way to switch between those modes at the document level via the DOCTYPE declaration.

Standards Mode

Under Standards Mode, browser rendering engines behave according to the letter of the standards. The CSS specifications are written to be backward compatible, so pages built to today's standards should not behave differently under some new specification 10 years from now.

In other words, yet-unwritten standards will not change how color works or how `font-family` designations are written even if they add features such as font embedding or new color keywords. In extreme cases—such as with the box model updates—a new property is created to designate new behaviors should be followed, but the default behaviors should match the old specifications.

Throughout this book I'll be discussing various properties and how they behave according to the W3C and thus in Standards Mode.

Almost Standards Mode

Almost Standards Mode was developed as a compromise between the stricter Standards Mode rendering and the implications of <img> being an inline element. Under Standards Mode, images had a space underneath them just as text does—the space for text is reserved for the descender of characters such as *g* and *q*. This caused images sliced up and then recombined inside a table-based layout to suddenly not match up as they were intended. Almost Standards Mode is identical to Standards Mode with the sole exception that it closes up the space underneath images.

Quirks Mode

Quirks Mode is a legacy rendering mode in some browsers that allows the browser to behave like a previous version of that browser. Quirks Mode, by definition, works differently in various web browsers and does not fully follow any CSS specification. It is useful mainly for letting old sites live on without the need for maintenance and for allowing code built to work only in a specific browser to continue working.

tip

Building new sites under Quirks Mode is difficult because of the behavior differences between browsers and the different ways they diverge from the CSS2 and CSS3 specifications. Stick with Standards Mode if you're building new sites, and forget that anything else exists.

Choosing Modes with a DOCTYPE Switch

At the time that browser vendors were implementing rendering modes, the Web was largely a mess of invalid tag-soup HTML4, browser-targeted code, and "best viewed in…" graphics. Only a few developers were writing valid code, reading specifications, and using DOCTYPES like those designating XHTML. This provided an opportunity to use the DOCTYPE declaration (or lack thereof) to indicate the type of code being written and therefore to switch between modes.

A missing or invalid DOCTYPE will put a browser into Quirks Mode, as will the following:

```
<!DOCTYPE HTML PUBLIC "-//W3C//DTD HTML 3.2 Final//EN">
<!DOCTYPE HTML PUBLIC "-//W3C//DTD HTML 4.01
➥ Transitional//EN">
```

The following will put browsers into Standards Mode or Almost Standards Mode:

```
<!DOCTYPE html>
<!DOCTYPE HTML PUBLIC "-//W3C//DTD HTML 4.01//EN"
➥ "http://www.w3.org/TR/html4/strict.dtd">
<!DOCTYPE html PUBLIC "-//W3C//DTD XHTML 1.0
➥ Transitional//EN">
```

The Wikipedia article on Quirks Mode (*http://en.wikipedia.org/wiki/Quirks_mode*) contains a more complete chart of behaviors.

X-UA-Compatible

Having just two modes is not enough for some, particularly those building closed or internal applications using web technologies. Microsoft has shown concern that changes or fixes to the browser will break already tested and deployed code in ways that DOCTYPE switching alone could not satisfy. The X-UA-Compatible header, when set via an HTTP header or `<meta>` tag, was introduced as a way to lock IE8 and beyond into behaving like a specific older version of the browser. The following example tells the browser that it should behave like IE8 in Standards Mode:

```
<meta http-equiv="X-UA-Compatible" content="IE=8" />
```

The next example tells the browser to emulate IE7 and use the DOCTYPE derived mode:

```
<meta http-equiv="X-UA-Compatible" content="IE=EmulateIE7" >
```

More background and examples of values for X-UA-Compatible are available from Microsoft (*http://msdn.microsoft.com/en-us/library/cc288325(VS.85).aspx*).

Specific Mode Differences

If you want to know more (and aren't content to just ignore that Quirks Mode exists at all), Jukka Korpela has a very detailed list of differences between Quirks Mode and Standards Mode in various browsers (*http://www.cs.tut.fi/~jkorpela/quirks-mode.html*). Peter-Paul Koch charted many of the differences in an easy-to-read table (*http://www.quirksmode.org/css/quirksmode.html*).

Targeting Browsers

In a perfect world, there would be no need to send or hide specific styles to specific browsers or find ways to accomplish something without CSS that there are clearly defined properties for. In the real world, you can get away with being almost perfect. Under Standards Mode rendering, sending different style rules to different browsers is not the norm, but some projects will require a small tweak here or there to pull a stray browser back into line.

Here I show three common ways to approach browser targeting and why they work. The first two are useful if you need to make minor changes, and the last is useful if you are making more regular changes, particularly if you have to develop for older versions of Internet Explorer.

Targeting with Selectors

The rules that browsers use to parse CSS selectors dictate that unknown syntaxes for selectors should cause the entire rule to be ignored. You can use that, combined with recent selectors that were not implemented in older browsers, to carefully craft rules for browsers. This can be one of the cleanest ways to target different features toward different editions of browsers or to offer fallback options for older browsers. You could write the following two CSS declarations:

```
html body { background-color: red; }
html>body { background-color: blue; }
```

Browsers that support the child selector will display a red background on the page, and those that do will display in blue.

Targeting with Syntax Hacks

Some browsers don't quite follow the same parsing rules and handle what would be considered an error or invalid syntax in a unique manner. Over time, web developers have stumbled upon (or gone on quests to find) these differences and used them as "hacks" in some form of browser targeting.

In the following example, most browsers will ignore the unknown property `_height`, but IE will instead ignore the _ character and consider it as a "height," giving you a way to send a different value to IE if needed.

```
div {
    height: 200px;
    _height: 300px;
}
```

If you want to target IE6 and older, you might use the `* html` hack, which to most browsers will not apply to any elements because there is no element above the root `<html>` tag, but IE got that wrong until version 7.

```
div.column {
   width: 200px;
}
* html div.column {
   width: 198px;
}
```

You can find a compendium of CSS hacks and their dangers on swik.net (*http://swik.net/CSS/CSS+Hacks*).

The danger in using hacks of any nature is that it is impossible to control how future browsers behave in the same circumstance. Will a future Safari version parse your hack the same way but no longer need the changed value you're feeding it? You're leveraging incomplete support for specifications (or more directly, software bugs), and therefore you're at the mercy of what fixes developers make over time.

Microsoft Conditional Comments

If you find you need to give a good deal of specialized code to Internet Explorer or that you don't want to mix and maintain selectors or syntax hacks, you can use conditional comments (*http://en.wikipedia.org/wiki/Conditional_comment*). Using standard HTML comments (because non-IE browsers will ignore anything inside of them) and a few extra characters that tell IE to pay attention, you can feed IE or some specific version of IE a link to a style sheet with extra rules.

```
<!--[if IE]>
<link type="stylesheet" src="/css/all_ie.css">
<![endif]-->
```

(continues on next page)

```
<!--[if lt IE 8]>
<link type="stylesheet" src="/css/ie_lessthan_8.css">
<![endif]-->
```

The downside to adding style rules in this manner is that you create two or three places where code for the same item resides, making it easy to forget to maintain each set of rules. A comment in the main CSS file designating where there is additional code can be a useful way to keep track of things:

```
#block { /* see also: @ie_lessthan_8.css */
    ...
}
```

The upside to conditional comments is that you have much greater control and confidence over what versions of IE will see your code than hacks can provide.

IE and hasLayout

In versions 6 and 7, Internet Explorer has an internal method of distinguishing when an element in the page needs some special layout features such as positioning or sizing. Based on the application of certain styles, such as height or positioning, Internet Explorer places an element into a bucket that gets extra layout handling or one that doesn't. This internal flag is labeled `hasLayout`. The `hasLayout` flag was not meant to be exposed to those of us building web sites, but the internal architecture that relies on this flag is also the source of a few common CSS bugs. **Figure 2.2** shows the indicator present on a `<div>` element in the IE Developer Toolbar.

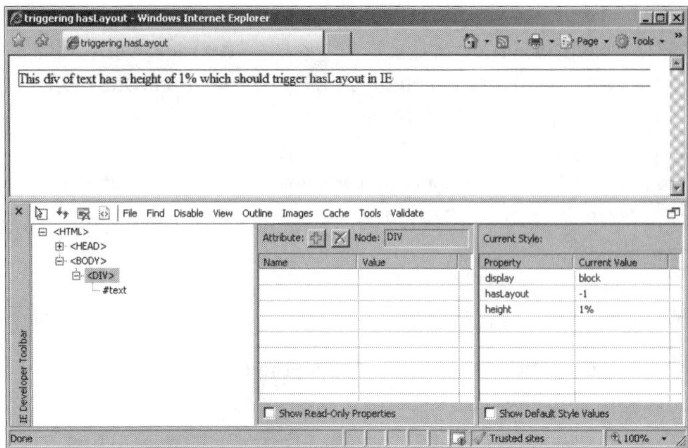

Figure 2.2 *An element with* hasLayout *revealed via the Developer Toolbar in IE7.*

Unfortunately, the distinction between an element that goes into the bucket that gets the extra internal presentation logic and one that doesn't leads to one of the most commonly attributed problem in Internet Explorer 6 and 7, called the Peekaboo bug.

The Peekaboo bug is so named because a block of content on a page may disappear (or flash in and out) while scrolling a page if the block does not have the hasLayout flag triggered. You can't set the hasLayout flag directly, but you can "force" it into the proper state by setting one of a number of CSS properties for the element, including the following:

```
div.columnA {
   height: 1%; /* trigger hasLayout by providing a dimension */
}
div.columnB {
   zoom: 1; /* trigger hasLayout by using this nonstandard
      property */
}
```

You can find an excellent discussion of `hasLayout` in "On having layout" (*http://www.satzansatz.de/cssd/onhavinglayout.html*), and Microsoft offers its own documentation on the property (*http://msdn.microsoft.com/en-us/library/bb250481(VS.85).aspx*).

IE8 still has the `hasLayout` property internally, though its effects on layout behavior are mostly resolved.

Browser Grading

In the previous sections, I outlined a few methods commonly used to work with web browsers, both old and new, to make sure they're handling your CSS properly and to target them when they don't.

But creating all these different versions of code for different browsers, testing them thoroughly, documenting them, and maintaining them over time can be time-consuming and frustrating.

By creating a tiered support matrix of browsers, you can save time in development and help communicate the technical requirements clearly to your client, other developers on the project, the QA team testing and approving your work, and those maintaining the site and handling customer feedback.

The specific breakdown of which browsers are most important and which browsers fit under other categories is a business decision that has to be made on a case-by-case basis. Yahoo!'s "Graded Browser Support" document (*http://developer.yahoo.com/yui/articles/gbs/index.html*) offers a well-reasoned explanation of YUI's grading methodology and results (**Figure 2.3**) and is a common example I turn to when on a new project or when educating others about the benefits of grading.

Figure 2.3
YUI A-grade browser matrix.

	Win XP	Win 7	Mac 10.5.†	Mac 10.6.†
Firefox 3.0.†	A-grade			
Firefox 3.6.†	A-grade	A-grade		A-grade
Chrome 4.0.†	A-grade			
IE 8.0	A-grade	A-grade		
IE 7.0	A-grade			
IE 6.0	A-grade			
Safari 4.0.†			A-grade	A-grade

This specific categorization works for the YUI developers but may not for you. Therefore, the following is a rough outline of the designations I have found to work for large commercial projects.

A-Grade Browsers

A-grade browsers represent the target platforms when deciding how to implement a site and what CSS tools and other technologies you can comfortably use. Browsers such as Firefox 3, Safari 4, and IE7 find their way into this classification based on their capabilities or the size of their user base.

B-Grade Browsers

B-grade browsers may be older versions of common browsers or current versions of browsers on uncommon operating systems or devices. These browsers may, but are not expected to, be able to display some CSS2 or CSS3 features or JavaScript tricks. However, the pages you build should still be tested in these browsers to make sure they are fully functional, they are accessible, your branding message comes across, and they don't appear to look "broken."

F-Grade Browsers

For the purposes of development, testing, and ongoing support, it may be useful to explicitly state which browsers or configurations will not be supported. Visitors with older browsers such as Netscape 6, Internet Explorer 5, or older mobile devices are *F-grade* browsers that will just get what they get and have to make due.

X-Grade Browsers

X-grade browsers are assumed to fall into the A-grade category but because of a small share of your user base or similarities to browsers already listed as A-grade, they aren't on your radar or testing matrix. Older point releases, Linux versions, or alternate UI browsers such as Camino or Flock that use the same rendering engines as A-grade browsers fit in this category.

A+-Grade Browsers

It is increasingly useful to have an extra category called *A+-grade* browsers defined to allow for some extra flair above and beyond the A-grade category. New CSS3 features such as rounded corners, animations, or transitions can be used to enhance the experience for some visitors while not being central to the site's design.

CSS Support via JavaScript

When you want to use the latest and greatest coding techniques on your web site and when your business needs or your user base dictates that you need an A- or B-grade level of support for a browser that otherwise isn't up to the task, it is common to use drop-in JavaScript libraries to bridge support or implement alternative methods of achieving a similar visual effect. This is a great way to ensure support for rounded corners via `border-radius` (Chapter 8) or make sure all of your selectors are understood.

I discuss specific examples of this type of script in Chapter 13.

A Practical Strategy

There are many factors that go into how a web page appears to a visitor—so many that it can be overwhelming if you attempt to understand and control them all. It is important to remember that ultimately it is your visitor and not you who is in control of their browsing experience. The only way to stay on budget, to stay on time, and to stay sane is to figure out what is important to make your site shine, then pick a method or methods to get you close to your goal in the most possible scenarios, and finally get comfortable with letting the rest go.

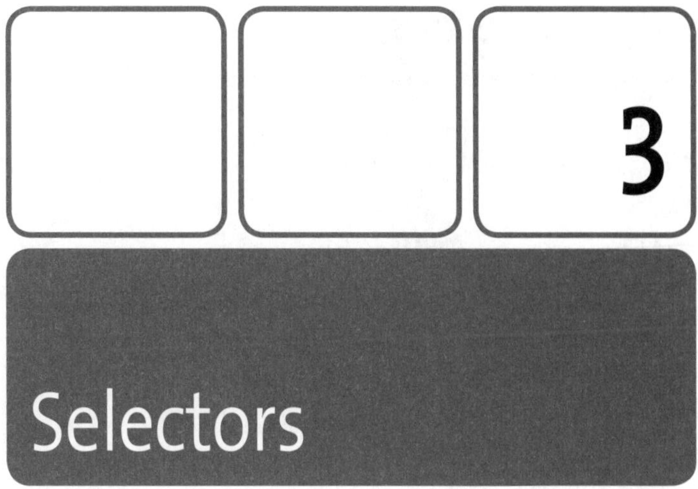

3 Selectors

You use selectors to define the elements on a page that you want to apply certain properties to. Elements in the document can be matched based on the HTML tag used, based on class or ID attributes, based on the relationship to other elements, or based on the current status in the document. You can also combine simple selectors to form a chain of conditions that must be met before the style rule is applied.

E (Type Selectors)

The type selector selects an element by its type.

```
h1 {} /* selects all h1 elements */
form {} /* selects all form elements */
```

* (Universal Selector)

The universal selector matches any element type in the document. It is implied if there is a sequence of other simple selectors and no specific type selector is present.

```
* {} /* selects all elements in a document */
*.thumb {} /* selects all elements with class thumb
   [see Class Selector below] */
.thumb {} /* same as previous, * is implied */
```

#id (ID Selector)

The ID selector matches any element with the specified value as its ID attribute.

```
#header {} /* selects the element with the ID of header */
*#header {} /* same as previous */
div#footer {} /* selects the div element with class footer */
```

.class (Class Selector)

The class selector matches elements with the specified class name. For elements whose `class` attribute contains multiple space-separated words, the class selector will select an element if *any* of those words match the specified class name.

```
.help {} /* matches all elements with a class of help */
img.thumbnail {} /* matches image elements with class of
   thumbnail */
```

Attribute Selectors

In addition to `id` and `class` attributes, any attribute can be used for selection with via attribute selectors.

[att]

Selects elements with the attribute `att`, regardless of the attribute's value.

```
input[required] {} /* matches html5 input elements with the
   required attribute */
```

[att=val]

Selects elements with the attribute `att` with the value equal to `val`.

```
a[rel=tag] {} /* matches anchors with the rel attribute equal
   to tag */
```

[att~=val]

Selects elements with the attribute att whose value includes the word val in its space-delimited list of words. (Think multiple class names.)

```
a[rel~=friend] {} /* matches anchors with copyright as one
   of many words in the rel attribute. For example, XFN's
   rel="met friend". */
```

[att|=val]

Selects elements with the attribute att whose value equals val or begins with val followed by the separator -. This is intended to be used to match the language subcode for the hreflang attribute.

```
*[hreflang|=en] {} /* matches all elements with hreflang en,
   en-us, en-au, and en-gb */
```

[att^=val]

Selects elements with the attribute att whose value begins with val. Added in CSS3.

```
a[href^=http] {} /* matches all links that begin with text
   "http" */
```

[att$=val]

Selects elements with the attribute att whose value ends with val. Added in CSS3.

```
a[href$=.pdf] {} /* matches all links to PDF files */
```

[att*=val]

Selects elements with the attribute att whose value contains the substring val anywhere within it. Added in CSS3.

```
input[id*=phone] {} /* matches all input fields with phone as
   part of the ID */
```

tip **Although ID and class attributes can be selected via the attribute selector, their more specialized selectors have been optimized by browser vendors and should be used instead.**

Pseudo-class Selectors

Pseudo-classes fall into two groups: dynamic pseudo-classes that represent a specific state the document or element is in (*visited* links) and structural pseudo-classes that represent information about an element's position in the document tree (the *first* list item).

`:link`, `:visited` (Link Pseudo-classes)

Links in a document have two states. When unvisited as determined by the browser and its document history, a link can be selected with the `:link` pseudo-class, or when visited, it can be selected via `:visited`.

```
a:link { color: blue; }
a:visited { color: purple; }
```

`:hover`, `:active`, `:focus` (Action Pseudo-classes)

The three interaction states of hovering, actively being clicked or used, and in focus can be independently styled using the `:hover`, `:active`, and `:focus` pseudo-classes.

note **The `:hover` pseudo-class for nonlink (<a>) elements is not supported in IE6 or earlier but is supported on links as of IE4.**

The LoVe/HAte of Hyperlink LVHA

Links can be in multiple states at the same time, and all pseudo-classes have identical specificity, so the order in which the link and action pseudo-classes are defined is important. The last one that applies at any given time will take precedence.

At the moment it is clicked, a previously visited link will match all five of these pseudo-classes. If `a:visited` is the last selector of the bunch, then those properties will be applied, and different properties defined for the hover or active states will never be seen.

The mnemonic device LoVe/HAte is a useful way to remember the proper order of selectors.

`:target` (Target Pseudo-class)

The target pseudo-class represents the element targeted by a named anchor in a URI such as the *top* in *http://example.com/index.html#top* (either by ID, or in the case of HTML4 a `name` attribute).

`:enabled`, `:disabled`, `:checked` (UI Pseudo-classes)

The `:enabled`, `:disabled`, and `:checked` pseudo-classes are used to target form elements in various states. Any form element can be either enabled or disabled, usually determined by the presence or lack of a `disabled` HTML attribute. Check box and radio button elements can also be `:checked` through user interaction or the checked attribute.

The CSS3 Basic User Interface specification has defined selectors for the additional user interface states of `:default`, `:valid`, `:invalid`, `:required`, `:optional`, `:in-range`, `:out-of-range`, `:read-only`, and `:read-write`. These selectors allow for the styling of the various states available with HTML5 form elements.

:lang() (Language Pseudo-class)

The language pseudo-class allows for selection based on the language of the text.

```
article:lang(en) {} /* selects an article element in English */
article:lang(es) {} /* selects an article element in Spanish */
```

note **This is different from selection based on `lang` or `hreflang` via the attribute selector because the language pseudo-class may be inherited from a parent element or defined as part of the document headers.**

:root (Root Element Pseudo-class)

The root element pseudo-class is a shortcut to select the root node of the document. For HTML documents, this is always the `html` element.

:nth-child(), :nth-last-child() (Nth Child Pseudo-classes)

These pseudo-class selectors match elements that appear at a specific position in a list of elements containing that list item and all its sibling elements. The position is defined via the pattern *an+b* where a and b are integers.

The values odd and even are shortcuts to select every odd (or 2n+1) or even (2n) item.

"Zebra striping" a list of items or successive rows of a table (**Figure 3.1** on the next page) can easily be accomplished via the nth-child pseudo-class without the need for additional class names or other hooks in the document markup.

```
tr { background-color: #FFF; color: #000; }
tr:nth-child(odd) { background-color: #AAA; }
```

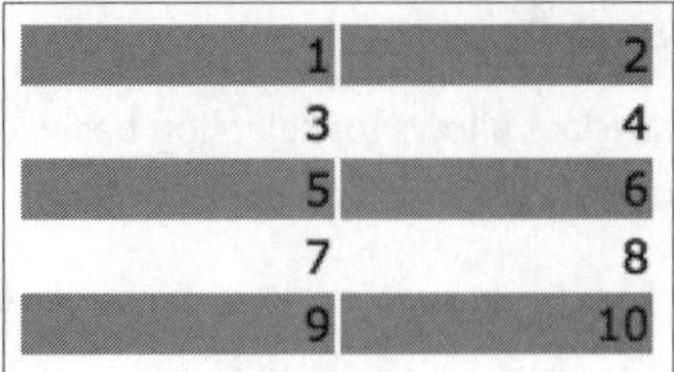

Figure 3.1
Zebra striping, or applying background colors to alternating table rows.

:first-child, :last-child (First and Last Child Pseudo-classes)

The first-child and last-child pseudo-class selectors represent the first and last children elements of some parent element. They are equivalent to `:nth-child(1)` and `:nth-last-child(1)`, respectively.

These selectors can be extremely useful for the common design pattern of using borders as a divider between a set of elements but not outside them (**Figure 3.2**).

```
li { border-top: 1px solid red; } /* place a border above all
   li elements */
li:first-child { border-top: none; } /* remove the border
   from the top of the first item */
```

Figure 3.2
Border on the first-child list item is removed.

Item 1
Item 2
Item 3
Item 4
Item 5
Item 6

Alternately, this can also be done via `:last-child`:

```
li { border-bottom: 1px solid red; } /* place a border above
   all li elements */
li:last-child { border-bottom: none; } /* remove the border
   from the bottom of the last item */
```

`:nth-of-type()`, `:nth-last-of-type()` (Nth of Type Pseudo-classes)

While `nth-child()` matches any element type, `nth-of-type()` and `nth-last-of-type()` select every *an+b* element where the set of elements is based on a collection of sibling elements that are *only* of the same element type.

One application of the nth-of-type selector is to set alternating styles on successive images found in a parent element regardless of what type of content is between them.

`:first-of-type`, `:last-of-type` (First and Last of Type Pseudo-classes)

Similarly to first-child and last child, there are the shortcuts `:first-of-type` and `:last-of-type`, which represent `:nth-of-type(1)` and `:nth-last-of-type(1)`, respectively.

`:only-child` (Only Child Pseudo-class)

This pseudo-class selects elements that are the only child of their parent element. Any element selected by `:only-child` matches both the `:first-child` and `:last-child` selectors.

:only-of-type (Only of Type Pseudo-class)

The only of type pseudo-class matches an element if it is the only element of its type among its sibling elements. That is, it matches both the `:first-of-type` and `:last-of-type` selectors.

:empty (Empty Pseudo-class)

The empty pseudo-class selects elements only when they contain no child nodes. This includes text nodes and whitespace characters.

```
td:empty { background-color: rgb(80%,80%,80%); } /* shade any
   empty table cells */
```

:not() (Negation Pseudo-class)

The negation pseudo-class allows you to select the case where elements do not match the provided simple selector.

```
p:not(.note) {} /* paragraph elements without the class note */
input:not(:required) {} /* optional input fields */
td:not(:nth-child(odd)) {} /* not odd, or the equivalent of
   :nth-child(even) */
```

Pseudo-element Selectors

Pseudo-elements are phantom elements that don't appear in the HTML document but instead represent a part of the document that the browser overlays on the document structure to represent properties of the layout. For example, because of differences in font sizes, line lengths, and devices, you cannot wrap the text that will appear on the first line of a paragraph of text in a <span> tag with much accuracy. However, browsers will place a phantom pseudo-element around just that first line of text as if you did.

note **CSS1 and CSS2 defined the first-letter, first-line, before, and after pseudo-elements with a single colon (:). To better distinguish pseudo-elements from pseudo-classes, the CSS3 spec has changed this to two colons (::). For those four original pseudo-elements, browsers should support both syntaxes. Other pseudo-elements can be written only with the double colon (::).**

`::first-letter` (First-Letter Pseudo-element)

This pseudo-element selects the first letter of a block or block-like element (table-cell, table-caption, inline-block, list-item). If block elements are nested, the first letter of the text will be matched via both elements.

```
div::first-letter { font-weight: bold; }
p::first-letter { color: blue; }
[...]
<div><p>First paragraph.</p><p>Second paragraph.</p></div>
```

Given this example, the *F* in the word *First* will be selected by both rules and be bold and blue, while the *S* in Second will just be blue.

A drop cap effect can be easily achieved by applying a left float and an increased font size to the first letter of a block.

`::first-line` (First-Line Pseudo-element)

The first-line pseudo-element selects the first line of a block or block-like element after the block has been formatted based on its context.

```
p::first-line { text-transform: uppercase; }
```

`::before`, `::after` (Before and After Pseudo-elements)

The before and after pseudo-elements are used to select generated content before or after an element. This content inherits properties from the element to which it is attached. The following would place the text *NOTE:* before any instance of `p.note` in the document.

```
p.note::before {
   content: "NOTE: ";
   font-weight: bold;
}
```

Chapter 10 covers generated content and the content property in more depth.

`::selection` (Selection)

The selection pseudo-element represents a virtual inline element that wraps any text selected by a visitor. With any selection, you can set a limited number of properties including the color and background color of the text.

```
::selection { color: black; background-color: yellow; }
```

note **The selection pseudo-element has been removed from the current CSS3 Selectors Module Recommendation but is implemented in some browsers as `::selection` and in Firefox and other Gecko browsers as `::-moz-selection`.**

Combinators or Relational Selectors

The selectors described to this point select elements based on an element type or the properties of an element. Combinators are used to combine these simple selectors in ways that describe document structure.

E F (Descendant Combinator)

Represented by whitespace, the descendant selector describes an element (F) that is contained within another element (E). The number of elements between the ancestor and descendant does not matter. As a result, the following selector will match all elements inside the document body:

```
body * {}
```

E>F (Child Combinator)

The child selector describes an element (F) that is the child (or direct descendant) of another element (E).

```
ul > li { font-family: san-serif; }
ol > li { font-family: monospace; }
```

Here, list items that are direct children of an unordered list tag will be in a sans-serif font, and those that are direct children of an ordered list will be fixed-width.

E+F (Adjacent Sibling Combinator)

The adjacent sibling combinatory matches elements (F) that come directly after other elements (E) and share the same parent element.

```
h1 + p { font-size: 1.2em }
```

This example will select all paragraphs that come directly after an <h1> tag and apply an increased font size.

E~F (General Sibling Combinator)

With this selector, the element (F) is selected if it appears at some point after its sibling element (E).

Combining and Chaining Selectors

Using combinators, you can chain together the individual selectors discussed earlier to create more complex selectors that can be used to describe elements not just in the entire document but in specific parts of the document or that match specific markup patterns. The following are all examples of chaining simple selectors:

```
nav ul li:first-child {}
.vevent h2+* {}
ul ul ul ul>li {}
#page .hentry a.entry-title:link {}
div#main form#registration fieldset
➥ input[type="text"]:invalid {}
```

Translating Selectors into Plain English

If it hasn't yet become clear, selectors can be read from left to right and described as traveling toward the top of the document tree. The selector `header ul>li` selects "any list item elements that are children of unordered list elements that are contained in a header element."

If you are ever unsure of what a selector does, the online tool SelectOracle (*http://gallery.theopalgroup.com/selectoracle/*) translates CSS2 and CSS3 selectors into English (or Spanish) for you.

Specificity

If the only thing that governed which property gets applied to an element is the order in which the selectors appear, working with CSS would be a never-ending battle of copying and pasting and rearranging code. Rules of specificity—how specific the description of the element in the selector is written—are used to help determine which properties will apply.

```
blockquote p { color: green; }
[...]
p { margin: 20px; color: black; }
```

In the previous code, all paragraph elements will have a 20-pixel margin on each side; however, because the selector matching paragraphs contained in `blockquote` elements is more specific, those will be the desired color green, even though the rule is found before the simple p selector.

Specificity is calculated by tallying grouping the simple selectors into three buckets, then tallying each of those buckets (a-b-c), and finally comparing the results to other competing rules. This is from the CSS3 Selectors Module (*http://www.w3.org/TR/css3-selectors/#specificity*):

> *A selector's specificity is calculated as follows:*
>
> - *count the number of ID selectors in the selector (= a)*
> - *count the number of class selectors, attributes selectors, and pseudo-classes in the selector (= b)*
> - *count the number of type selectors and pseudo-elements in the selector (= c)*
> - *ignore the universal selector*

Selectors inside the negation pseudo-class are counted like any other, but the negation itself does not count as a pseudo-class.

Concatenating the three numbers a-b-c (in a number system with a large base) gives the specificity.

You might have gotten lost somewhere around "in a number system with a large base," and I wouldn't blame you. Looking at a few examples should clear things up:

```
#user { color: rgb(1,1,1); } /* a=1 b=0 c=0 */
#user:first-child { color: rgb(2,2,2); } /* a=1 b=1 c=0 */
div div+div div div+div div div div>div div div:first-child {
   color: rgb(3,3,3);
} /* a=0 b=0 c=13 */
div.foo { color: rgb(4,4,4); } /* a=0 b=1 c=1 */
.foo .foo+.foo .foo+.foo .foo .foo .foo .foo>.foo .foo
➥.foo:first-child {
   color: rgb(5,5,5);
} /* a=0 b=12 c=1 */
.foo.bar { color: rgb(6,6,6); } /* a=0 b=2 c=0 */
[id="user"] { color: rgb(7,7,7); } /* a=0 b=1 c=0 */
```

If all these selectors matched the same element in a complex HTML document, the text in that element would be the color `rgb(2,2,2)`. Though some of the selectors, particularly the third and fourth, are more verbose then others, the second is considered the one with the greatest specificity.

The bit about concatenating the number in a non-decimal-based number system is a reminder that when combining the results, you need to compare them as buckets. For example, compare [1][1][0] vs. [0][12][1] instead of 110 vs. 121.

note **It may be counterintuitive, but the ID selector #user in the previous example is more specific than selecting the same element using the attribute selector `[id=user]`.**

The `!important` Declaration

There are occasions where neither the source order nor the specificity can be changed, but you still need a way to trump the specificity calculations. In these cases, you can use the `!important` declaration to lock down individual properties.

```
blockquote p { color: green; }
[...]
p { color: black !important; }
```

Here specificity and source order are ignored, and the text will be black, not green.

tip **Most projects will never need to use the `!important` declaration. If you find yourself putting it in your code to make something work, instead take another look at what selectors you are using, source order, and whether including certain CSS code on a page is necessary. The use cases for this declaration typically arise when working with third-party code, content management systems, or other situations where you do not have the ability to rethink selectors.**

Selector Strategies

There are an infinite number of ways you can write selectors, and there are often dozens of ways a particular element in a document can be selected. Well-written and easily maintainable CSS often comes down to choosing selectors that are just verbose enough to offer the specificity and distinctions you need to style the various elements of a site.

Browser Support for Selectors

Browser support for the selectors described in this chapter is great in some cases and just starting to get there for other cases. Selectors such as type, ID, class, and links are supported everywhere. CSS2 and CSS3 selectors such as attributes and some of the combinators such as + and > are supported widely enough to be useful on many projects. Peter-Paul Koch maintains some useful support charts for selectors in desktop browsers (*http://www.quirksmode.org/css/contents.html*) and mobile browsers (*http://www.quirksmode.org/m/css.html*).

Grouping Selectors

Different selectors can be separated by a comma and be assigned the same properties. This will allow you to cut down on repeated use of the same properties, keep your layouts more uniform, and make changes and small tweaks easier.

```
p, blockquote, ul, li, dl {
   padding: 0;
   margin: 0 1em 1.5em;
}
```

This statement gives many block-level elements that may appear in the content areas of your document the same whitespace.

Selector Speed

The greater the complexity of selectors, in the form of chaining multiple nodes or using sibling combinators or attribute selectors, the harder the rendering engine needs to work when parsing the document and drawing the page. Speed that is measured in milliseconds may not seem like a factor in the performance of a web site, but tallied over a large document, and in particular when JavaScript is used to alter the DOM structure, the complexity and performance of selectors can be noticeable when animating multiple items or doing other complex tasks.

tip **If the document is using JavaScript to manipulate the DOM or Ajax calls to add new content to the document after it loads, the impact of complex selectors or changes far up the document tree may make the speed of complex selectors more noticeable.**

Selector Readability

Sometimes selectors or groups of selectors are chosen for their readability and ease of scanning and visually chunking code in the style sheet document. More verbose selectors can easily be read and matched to elements in the HTML document structure. The following example takes that to an extreme:

```
html body section article h1 {}
html body section article p {}
html body section article ul {}
html body section article ul.compact li {}
html body section#opener article h1 {}
html body sidebar form#newsletter fieldset label {}
```

Although it is clear how these selectors match to a given HTML DOM, the selectors can be both slow and overly specific.

Selector Reusability

Keeping the pluses and minus of the other strategies in mind, it is often useful to write complex selectors with an eye toward common markup patterns and future reuse.

Start with good defaults for your simple type selectors to form a baseline that will make elements behave consistently regardless of where they appear.

Then chunk more specific selectors by their location in the DOM or what makes them unique, being just as verbose as you need to be to describe and group the selectors and being specific enough to override the defaults.

A selector such as `div.header div form#quickSearch input[type=submit]` may be more specific than you need for the current site and cannot be easily transferred to the next project you work on. Trimming the selector to `#quickSearch submit` may still provide the specificity and readability you need while being generic enough to reuse it.

```
#quickSearch label {}
#quickSearch input[type=text] {}
#quickSearch input[type=submit] {}
aside #quickSearch label {} /* adjust the properties for a
   special case */
```

4

Measurements, URLs, and Color Units

In the discussion of CSS syntax in Chapter 1, you saw that the second part of each CSS declaration is a value. In this chapter, you'll explore some common units for defining sizes (`<length>` and `<percentage>`), colors (`<color>`), and URLs (`<url>`) for defining these values.

Measurements

Dimensions and other measurements, such as `font-size`, are not just raw numbers but a number of some specified of units of measure. CSS has quite a variety of measurement units; the most commonly used are outlined in the following sections.

Pixels (px)

```
img.thumbnail { width: 150px; }
div { border-width: 3px; }
```

A pixel unit (`<length>`) is a fixed measurement based on the size of a common pixel.

note **Pixel units are not always a "pixel" or "dot" but are defined as a relative length measurement based on the given display. High-resolution media such as print will output 1px as multiple physical dots, and high-resolution devices such as the 326-dpi iPhone 4 will render a px unit at an appropriate size.**

Ems (em)

```
h1 { font-size: 1.6em; } /* make h1 font larger than base */
blockquote { width: 20em; } /* keep block readable */
```

One em unit (`<length>`) is a relative unit that equates to the font size of the element. When applied to the `font-size` property of an element, an em unit is relative to the parent element's font size. This behavior makes it useful for keeping the font size for emphasis, headers, and other tags relative to the base font sizing. It's also useful when applied to dimensions as a way to control readability and line lengths.

Points (pt)

```
body { font-size: 12pt; }
```

Points are an absolute length–based unit (<length>) equal to 1/72 of an inch. Points can be useful when setting type sizes for print and similar media where physical measurements may be stressed. On screen and mobile media, points are approximated based on the resolution of the display and the system settings, and working with px or em units can lead to more consistent results.

Percentages (%)

```
.column1 { width: 30%; } /* 30% of the containing block
   width */
p { line-height: 140%; } /* 140% of the font-size of the
   element */
p.note { font-size: 90%; } /* 90% of the parent's
   font-size */
```

Percentage-based units (<percentage>) are relative to another measurement. Percentages can be greater than 100 percent. Which measurement the value relates to is defined on a case-by-case basis; the previous code lines show some examples.

Percentage Calculations and the Box Model

50% + 50% = 100%

30% + 30% + 40% = 100%

Correct?

Sometimes it isn't. Because of rounding in the calculations involved in finding the percentage of the measurement it relates to, there may be an extra pixel or two to account for. Internet Explorer 6 is notorious for calculations that result in extra pixels and, as a result, for columns that don't fit into a space you think they should.

You can find more about layouts and the box model in Chapter 5.

Other Units of Note

Points are considered an *absolute length*–based units: They correspond to a physical measurement of 1/72 of an inch (approximated by the browser and device). Other absolute units include `in` (inches), `cm` (centimeters), `mm` (millimeters), and `pc` (picas, or 12pts).

Pixels and ems are *relative length*–based units: They are relative to some other measurement. Like `em`, the `ex` unit is relative to the size of the font (the *ex-height* or height of the character "x"). CSS3 has defined some other interesting relative length units such as the following: `rem` (relative to the font size of the root element) and `vw` and `vh` (relative to the viewport width and height, respectively). These units are just starting to be supported in previews of the next generation of browsers but are something to look forward to using.

URLs

The URL function (<url>) is used to designate the address of a resource for use in a property such as background-image or list-style-image. The path of the resource follows the same rules as other uniform resource identifier (URI) usages like link href values in HTML. When using external style sheet documents, relative paths relate to the document the CSS rule is found in (the external CSS document) and not the source HTML document.

```
body { background-image: url(../images/bg_body.png); }
body { background-image: url(/images/bg_body.png); }
body { background-image: url(http://example.com/images/
➥bg_body.png); }
```

URIs can be quoted with single or double quotes or can be left unquoted. For historical reasons dating back to IE for the Mac, single quotes are sometimes avoided as a best practice.

data: URIs

The data: URI scheme uses encoded strings to represent file data inline rather than as a path to an external file. This can be quite useful for small resources such as iconography, list bullets, or font faces because it cuts down the number of requests to the server or for mobile applications.

```
data:[<mediatype>][;base64],<data>
```

You can find support for this URI scheme in CSS in Internet Explorer 8+, Firefox, Safari, and Opera. The source code for data: URIs can be easily generated with "The data: URI kitchen" tool by Ian Hickson (*http://software.hixie.ch/utilities/cgi/data/data*).

Basic Colors

The following color units (<color>) define several different ways to designate solid colors and can be used for properties like text color, background-color, and border-color.

#rrggbb or #rgb

In hexadecimal notation, colors are represented by three sets of hexadecimal values (base-16), with the first set representing the red (r) value, the second representing the green (g) value, and the next representing the blue (b) value based on how displays add light to create the colors you see. A value of #000000 represents no light (black), #ffffff represents the most light (white), and #ff0000 represents only red light (bright red).

```
body { background-color: #999; } /* middle gray */
```

#rgb is a shorthand for #rrggbb, which is available to use when the two r characters match, the two g characters match, and the two b characters match (#a3b is equivalent to #aa33bb).

rgb(r,g,b)

You can also define RGB colors using decimal notation (sometimes called *functional notation*) along the same 256-step range (0 to 255) that the hexadecimal values represented. Each value can also be defined as a percentage of that 256-step range.

```
body { background-color: rgb(153,153,153); } /* middle
   gray */
body { background-color: rgb(60%,60%,60%); } /* middle
   gray */
```

note **You cannot mix integers and percentages in the same color unit designation. White is `rgb(255,255,255)` or `rgb(100%,100%,100%)`, but not `rgb(255,100%,255)`.**

hsl(h,s,l)

The hue-saturation-lightness color scheme offers a way to look at the color wheel that can be more intuitive when working with colors of a similar hue or tonality. Hue (h) is a number from 0 to 360 representing a radial position on the color wheel (0 or 360=red, 120=green, 240=blue). Saturation (s) is a percentage value from 0 to 100 percent with values closer to 0 percent approaching desaturated, or gray. Lightness (`l`) is again a percentage value from 0 to 100 percent, where 0 percent is black and 100 percent is white.

```
.error { border-color: hsl(0, 75%, 38%); } /* a muted red */
```

A chart of HSL colors in the CSS3 Color Module specification (*http://www.w3.org/TR/css3-color/#hsl-examples*) illustrates how the three scales work together to create colors.

Color Keywords

The HTML 4 specification defined the following 16 color keywords and their corresponding hex values: `aqua`, `black`, `blue`, `fuchsia`, `gray`, `green`, `lime`, `maroon`, `navy`, `olive`, `purple`, `red`, `silver`, `teal`, `white`, and `yellow`. Keywords are case insensitive and are not placed between quotes.

```
body { color: red; }
```

Several (131 to be exact) more commonly supported color keywords, such as `pink`, `plum`, `deepskyblue`, and `firebrick`, originally defined in the SVG specification, were added in CSS3, bringing the number of color keywords to 147.

Many Ways to Say the Same Thing

The following are all ways to set the same text color for a paragraph element in your document:

```
p { color: #fff; }
p { color: #ffffff; }
p { color: rgb(255,255,255); }
p { color: rgb(100%,100%,100%); }
p { color: hsl(0,0%,100%); }
p { color: white; }
```

The notation you choose to work with can depend on many factors. Your familiarity with the different color systems, which is the easiest to transpose from your favorite graphics application uses, or how the color palette for the site is designed all should impact this decision. With `hsl()`, it can be easier to write transitions via JavaScript, but watch for browser support issues since it's also the newest method of defining color.

Color with Alpha Transparency

CSS3 defines the ability to add a level of transparency to the otherwise solid color designation. Applying alpha transparency to borders, text colors, or backgrounds allows the color of the elements behind the targeted element to bleed through or combine with what is behind it. **Figure 4.1** shows the use of a transparent background color to mute the distractions created by a background image so that text can be readable.

The transparency in the color applies only to the parts of the element that color applies to and does not affect the transparency of elements it may contain or other objects like images. I discuss the `opacity` property, which applies to the visibility of an entire element, in Chapter 6.

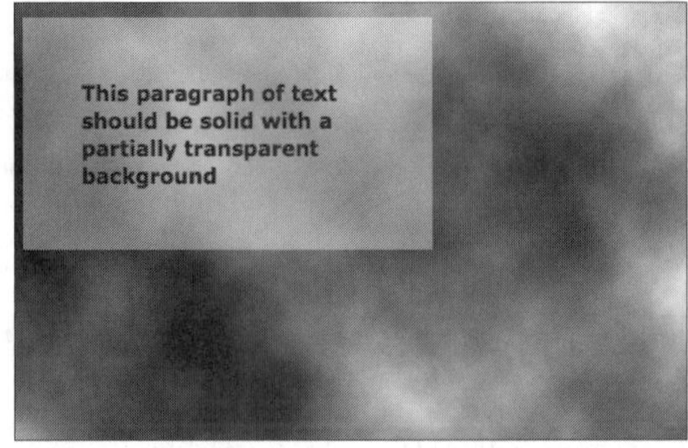

This paragraph of text
should be solid with a
partially transparent
background

Figure 4.1
Using a transparent background color to make solid text more readable against a background image.

rgba(r,g,b,a)

The r, g, and b values work on the same scale as their rgb() unit counterparts discussed earlier in this chapter. The alpha (a) value is a decimal number from 0 to 1, with 0 being completely transparent and 1 being fully opaque.

```
section { background-color: rgba(0,200,0,0.1); } /* very
   transparent green */
```

tip **Color units with alpha values of 1 are equivalent to using the solid color unit. Consider using that solid color unit instead because it may be supported by more browsers.**

hsla(h,s,l,a)

Like rgba(), hsla() is the same color as hsl() with an added designation for alpha transparency. This unit is also a decimal number from 0 to 1.

```
a { background-color: rgba(0,0,0,0.9); } /* almost solid
   black */
```

transparent

The `transparent` color keyword represents a color value that is fully transparent (and thus red channel or hue designations don't matter). You can think of it as a shorthand form for (and gets computed in browsers as) `rgba(0,0,0,0)`.

rgba() and hsla() Colors with Non-CSS3 Browsers

Colors units with alpha channels are supported in recent versions of Safari, Firefox, Opera, and the upcoming IE9. Browsers that don't support these units will skip them entirely because the `rgba()` or `hsla()` notation is as foreign to them as `madeupscheme()` is. This means if you defined an element's background to be "blue but a little transparent," the browser will not fall back to "blue but not transparent" and instead use whatever the previously defined or inherited color may be. If you want the fallback to be "blue but not transparent," you can write the rule set as follows:

```
div {
    background-color: rgb(0,0,255);
    background-color: rgba(0,0,255,90%);
}
```

All browsers will read the first `background-color` declaration. Browsers with `rgba()` support will then override that setting with the second declaration, while others will ignore it as invalid syntax.

As a variation on this method, if your layout calls for transparent red against white, resulting in a pink color, you might use that resulting color in the first declaration instead of a deeper red.

Creating and Maintaining Color Palettes

Defining a color palette for use in a web site and sticking to that set of color values can be a useful tool for styling new elements on a site, providing a consistent appearance throughout a site, and making it easy to find color values when making site changes.

Design

Color theory is far outside the scope of this book and is something you could study for years; however, here are a few tips for choosing the color scheme for a web site:

- Design applications such as Adobe Photoshop offer a detailed color picker that can be switched between RGB, HSL, and other color systems, making for easy translations into CSS units.
- Adobe Kuler is a tool for creating, browsing, and bookmarking color swatches from your browser or your desktop. You can make swatches based on a color wheel or drawn from an uploaded image file (*http://kuler.adobe.com/*).

Maintenance

Maintaining consistent color usage across a large amount of CSS code can sometimes be difficult. Color units are defined in so many different declarations across so many different elements that it is easy to keep the shade of gray being used the same or know what color should be used for links. Here are some hits for making the task easier:

- Pick one color unit type, and stick with it so searching for a color when it is time to change it is easier. Don't use `#ff0000`, `rgb(100%,0,0)` and the keyword `red` interchangeably.

- Maintain a style guide that lists all the colors used on the site along with the preferred unit value to represent them, and use only these colors.
- For complex or very large sites, consider using a CSS preprocessor like those discussed in Chapter 13 that allow you to define placeholders for color values and define a specific color value only once in your code.

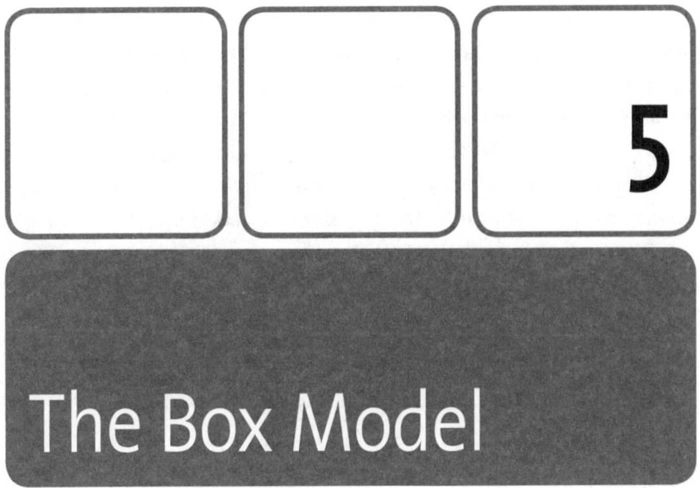

5 The Box Model

The space a block-level element takes up in a layout is controlled by the values of the height, width, margins, padding, and border properties. The description of how these properties interact and how those calculations are made is called the *box model*.

In the standard box model (`content-box`), the padding, borders, and margins of an element are added to the width and height of that element to determine the space it occupies in the layout. **Figure 5.1** displays a diagram of the box model as found in the CSS2.1 specification (*http://www.w3.org/TR/CSS21/box.html*). The additive process where width or height is not inclusive and thus the total size an element takes up may feel counterintuitive to some, but this works well when nesting elements or working with content such as images or video where you don't want to encroach on the content area.

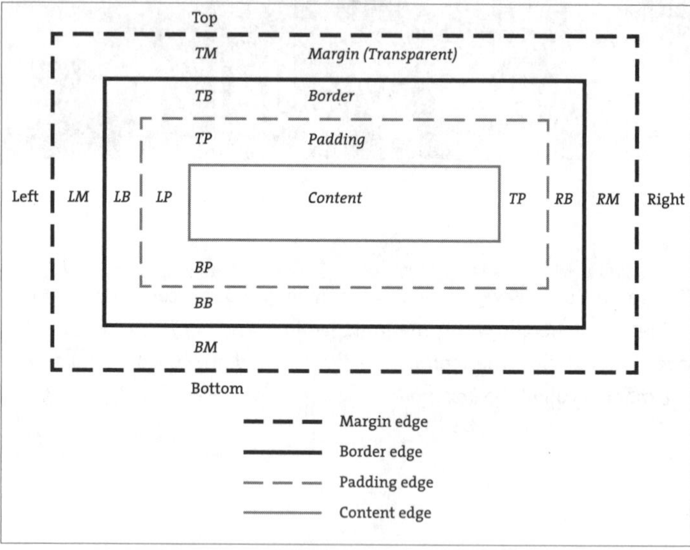

Figure 5.1 *The standard box model. The T, R, B, and L abbreviations represent the top, right, bottom, and left values of each property.*

Properties

`width`

The `width` property defines the width of an element.

- `<length>`: The width will be a fixed dimension.
- `<percentage>`: The width will be a percentage of the containing block's width.
- `auto`: The width will be calculated based on the available horizontal space (default).

`height`

The `height` property sets the height of an element.

- `<length>`: The height will be a fixed dimension.
- `<percentage>`: The height will be a percentage of the containing block's specified height; this is the equivalent of `auto` if no containing block height was specified.
- `auto`: The height will be calculated to fit the available content (default).

`margin`

The `margin` property sets the four margins surrounding an element. Each side may take one of the following property values:

- `<length>`: The margins will be a fixed dimension.
- `<percentage>`: The margins will be a percentage of the containing block's width (applies for margins in the vertical as well as horizontal directions).
- `auto`: For the left and right margins, `auto` is calculated to be the length needed to reach the containing element's sides; for the top and bottom, it is calculated as 0.

```
margin-top: 1px;
margin-right: 20%;
margin-bottom: 0;
margin-left: 40px;
margin: 2em; /* shorthand: all sides */
margin: 2em 0; /* shorthand: top & bottom; right & left */
margin: 2em 0 1em; /* shorthand: top; right & left; bottom */
margin: 2em 0 1em 10px;  /* shorthand: top; right; bottom;
   left */
```

When margins from two elements contact each other on a page, they "collapse" into one another with the resulting effect that the margin between each element is the size of the largest of the two margin properties. For example, if there is an <h2> with a bottom margin of 20 pixels followed by a paragraph with a top margin of 10 pixels, the space between the two elements will be 20 pixels, not 30.

padding

The `padding` property sets the four padding dimensions between an element's content area and its border. Each side may take one of the following values:

- `<length>`: The length will be a fixed dimension.
- `<percentage>`: The length will be a percentage of the containing block's width (applies for margins in the vertical as well as horizontal directions).

```
padding-top: 1px;
padding-right: 20%;
padding-bottom: 0;
padding-left: 40px;
```

```
padding: 2em; /* shorthand: all sides */
padding: 2em 0; /* shorthand: top & bottom; right & left */
padding: 2em 0 1em; /* shorthand: top; right & left; bottom */
padding: 2em 0 1em 10px;  /* shorthand: top; right; bottom;
   left */
```

border-width

The `border-width` property sets the size of an element's border.

- `<length>`: The border width will be a fixed dimension.
- `thin` | `medium` | `thick`: The border width is designated by keywords representing three border lengths of progressive thickness (not often used because of the inconsistency in definition of actual dimensions).

The `border-width` property defines the width of the border on an element. Like `margin` and `padding`, `border-width` is a shortcut for defining the four individual sides independently and can take one to four values.

```
border-top-width: 2px;
border-right-width: 0;
border-bottom-width: 10px;
border-left-width: 1px;
border-width: 2px 0 10px 1px;  /* shorthand: top; right;
   bottom; left */
```

In Chapter 8, I discuss some of the visual options for borders in detail, but only `border-width` impacts the dimensions of an element.

overflow

The `overflow` property defines what is done if the content in a box is too big for its defined space. The possible values for the `overflow` property are as follows:

- `visible`: Shows the content outside of the box (default)
- `hidden`: Clips the content and hides what falls outside the dimensions of the box
- `scroll`: Clips the content and always draws scrollbars to allow for access to additional content
- `auto`: Clips the content and draws scrollbars only when they are needed

The overflow behavior for the width and the height of a box can be individually set with the `overflow-x` and `overflow-y` properties.

note **By default, Internet Explorer will not let the content flow out of the box but instead expand the box to fit the content as if `width` or `height` were `min-width` or `min-height`. This is partly why a short height is used in the hasLayout fixes discussed in Chapter 2.**

Min and Max Dimensions

When designing flexible layouts or taking multiple types of devices into account, it can be useful to place restrictions on the size of elements. As you will see in Chapter 7, these properties are most useful when paired with width or height settings of `auto` or a different type of length unit.

```
article {
   width: 100%; /* let element fit parent */
   min-width: 200px; /* ensure content isn't too narrow */
   max-width: 900px /* ensure content isn't too wide */
}
```

- `min-width`: The minimum width of an element
- `max-width`: The maximum width of an element
- `min-height`: The minimum height of an element
- `max-height`: The maximum height of an element

Nesting Elements

When nesting HTML elements, the inner element's box is drawn inside the content area of the outer element. This results in an assortment of ways you can combine the properties to achieve the same visual effect or whitespace. As you nest elements, you compound the buildup of properties along the elements at the edge of these boxes.

To create the simple illustration shown in **Figure 5.2** from the nested elements `<div><div></div></div>`, you have a number of possibilities as to how you split the 100-pixel gray area between the outer element border area and the inner element's content area. That 100 pixels can be split however you'd like between the adjacent padding-margin-border area. Depending on that choice, it may be possible to create the 50-pixel inner white area with the inside border padding.

Figure 5.2
Content area surrounded by 50 pixels of white and then surrounded by 100 pixels of gray.

Example 1:

```
div {
   margin: 0;
   padding: 50px;
   border: 1px solid #999;
   background: #ccc;
}
div div {
   margin: 50px;
   padding: 50px;
   border: none;
   background: #fff;
}
```

Example 2:

```
div {
   margin: 0;
   padding: 100px;
   border: 1px solid #999;
   background: #ccc;
}
div div {
   margin: 0;
   padding: 0;
   border: 50px solid #fff;
   background: #fff;
}
```

Example 3:

```
div {
    margin: 0;
    padding: 75px;
    border: 1px solid #999;
    background: #ccc;
}
div div {
    margin: 25px;
    padding: 40px;
    border: 10px solid #fff;
    background: #fff;
}
```

Which element is best to style in a given situation can often be determined by evaluating the context and content needs. It will usually be obvious which element to use because you'll want to reserve one of the other elements or properties for other things, or you know that the style will be reused and should be applied to a container or other reused element.

Gutters surrounding text and other content are often best created by setting padding on the outer element. This will ensure the gutters are set to a consistent size regardless of the content within the container. It is more flexible and more easily maintained than the alternative of setting the left and right margin or padding on any possible child of that container.

In the next section, you'll see how using the box properties of a unique child element might be more practical.

Using Negative Margins

Margins can be a negative length as well as positive. Negative margins are an often overlooked but extremely useful device for manipulating the space between elements or for escaping the confines of the content area of a containing element.

The first example (**Figure 5.3**) overlaps two sibling elements by using a negative top margin.

Figure 5.3 *Negative top margin causing elements to overlay.*

Header Content

More Header Content

Some article content which will break into the header above

Some content of another article which will follow as normal

```
header {
   background: #999;
   padding-bottom: 2em;
}
article {
   border: 1px solid #999;
   background: #fff;
   margin: 1em 2em;
}
header+article {
   margin-top: -1em;
}
[...]
<header>
```

```
    <h1>Header Content</h1>
    <p>More Header Content</p>
</header>
<article>
    <p>Some article content which will break into the header
    above</p>
</article>
<article>
    <p>Some content of another article which will follow as
    normal</p>
</article>
```

In the second example (**Figure 5.4**), negative margins are used to bleed into the gutter provided by a 50-pixel padding on the containing element.

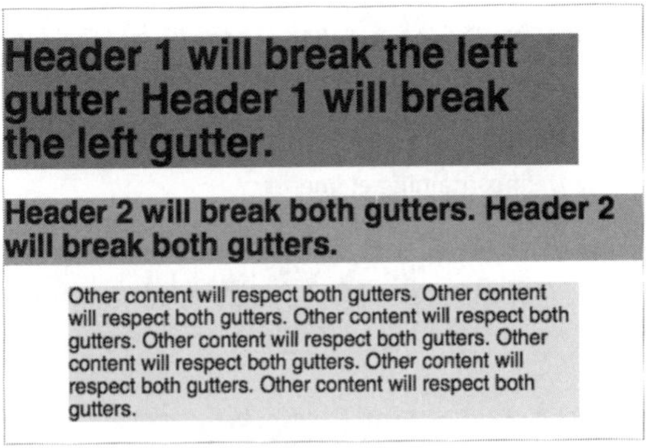

Figure 5.4 *Negative margins causing element to enter its parent's padding area.*

Header 1 will break the left gutter. Header 1 will break the left gutter.

Header 2 will break both gutters. Header 2 will break both gutters.

Other content will respect both gutters. Other content will respect both gutters. Other content will respect both gutters. Other content will respect both gutters. Other content will respect both gutters. Other content will respect both gutters.

```
div {
    width: 400px;
    padding: 0 50px;
}
```

(continues on next page)

```
div h1 {
   margin-left: -50px;
   background: #999;
}
div h2 {
   margin: 0 -50px;
   background: #CCC;
}
[...]
<div>
   <h1>Header 1 will break the left gutter</h1>
   <h2>Header 2 will break both gutters</h2>
   <p>Paragraph will respect both gutters</p>
</div>
```

Horizontal Centering Blocks

There is a subtlety in the definition of the auto value for the left and right margins that allows it to be used to center or right align blocks inside their containing elements.

```
<div>
   <p style="margin: 0 0 0 0;">margin: 0 0 0 0;</p>
</div>
<div>
   <p style="margin: 0 auto 0 0;">margin: 0 auto 0 0;</p>
</div>
<div>
   <p style="margin: 0 auto 0 auto;">margin: 0 auto 0 auto;
   </p>
</div>
```

```
<div>
   <p style="margin: 0 0 0 auto;">margin: 0 0 0 auto;</p>
</div>
```

Take a container <div> that is 500 pixels wide, as shown in **Figure 5.5**. If a 300-pixel wide <p> is inside that container, then you have 200 pixels of room to spare. If both margins on the <p> are 0, then the paragraph will be flush left. However, the definition of an auto margin value is that it will fill the container. A right margin of auto and left of 0 will not particularly change anything in the layout (the empty space is still on the right), but having both right and left margins set to `auto` will cause the space to be split between the two margins, and the <p> will appear centered just as if you had done the calculations yourself and set the margins to 100 pixels each.

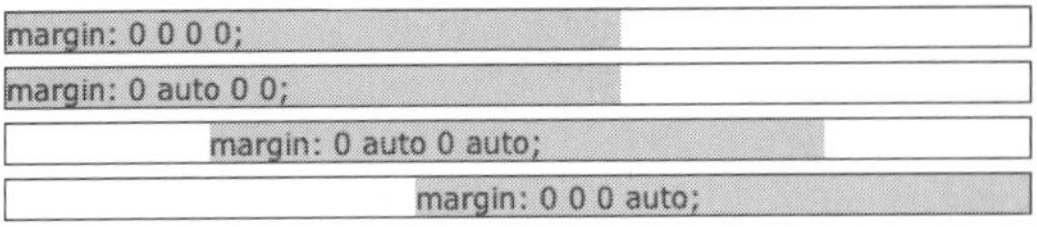

Figure 5.5 *Auto margin examples.*

```
margin: 0 0 0 0;
margin: 0 auto 0 0;
margin: 0 auto 0 auto;
margin: 0 0 0 auto;
```

An Alternative Box Model

In some Quirks Mode scenarios or if set via the `box-sizing` property introduced in CSS3, an element's padding and border are drawn *inside* the width and height, taking space away from the content area.

box-sizing

The box model used when calculating and placing borders and padding areas can be set using the `box-sizing` property.

- `content-box`: The width and height dimensions refer to the content area with padding and borders drawn outside (default).

- `border-box`: The width and height dimensions contain the border and padding as well as the content of the element, while an element's margins continue to fall outside of this area.

tip **Although using `box-sizing: border-box` may sometimes seem appealing (such as when mixing a percentage-based width and pixel-based border), this box-sizing model may cause confusion and difficulty when mixing with code written by others or working with a team of developers accustomed to the standard content-box behavior.**

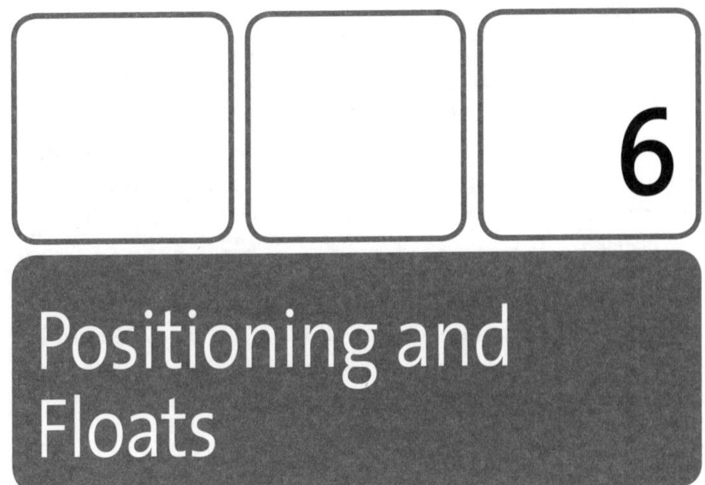

Positioning and Floats

Chapter 5 covered how block-level elements are given their shape and size. Before jumping headfirst into creating multicolumn layouts with these blocks, you need to learn how to position elements in your documents in relationship to the other items on a page.

The Document Flow

Reading content in an HTML document, without any JavaScript or CSS applied, is a top-down and left-to-right affair. Block elements take up the entire width of the document and follow one after another with their inline content flowing inside them. Margins and padding may alter the look or spacing some, but they alone do not change the positioning of the elements.

You have three ways to change the default positioning and interaction between elements in the top-down blob of content: You can force an element to behave like a different type of element, you can pull the item out of the flow completely, or you can pull the item to the side of its container and allow other items to wrap around it.

`display`

The `display` property is the key to the entire layout castle. I've already covered block elements and inline elements, but you need a number of other element types to define all the content that might display on a web page, including the following:

- `inline`: Creates one or more inline boxes, the familiar inline content
- `block`: Creates a block box
- `inline-block`: Creates a block box that behaves like an inline box, similar to the image (replaced element) behavior
- `list-item`: Creates a block box for the content and the list item marker
- `table`, `table-row`, `table-caption`: Creates three of the types of elements needed to present a table (Chapter 10)

- none: Removes the element from the presentation entirely, drawing no box of any kind

Alternating elements between the trio of `inline`, `block`, and none is sufficient for most design tasks, and as luck would have it, they are also the most widely supported values.

Position

The positioning of an element is based on the length of the box offset parameters: `top`, `right`, `bottom`, and `left`. Typically, `top` and `left` will be used for positioning elements since the top-left corner of the item being measured from—the beginning of a box—is easily understood in normal document flows.

static

`static` is the default value where an element is rendered in the normal flow and not uniquely positioned. The positioning parameters `top`, `right`, `bottom`, and `left` do not apply.

relative

In relative positioning, an element's position is calculated as normal, and then the offset positioning is applied relative to this normal position. Relative positioning does not take the element out of the normal flow, which leaves a space behind in the element's original position.

A relative positioned element with box offsets set to 0 (or undefined) will appear in its normal position; however, it will create a new point of origin for any of its child elements that may be positioned absolutely.

absolute

Absolute positioning takes the element out of the normal document flow—collapsing any space it may have otherwise used—and positions it in relation to the origin point created by the last-positioned containing block.

The code used for **Figure 6.1** demonstrates how to use absolute positioning to place elements at the four corners of its containing element.

Figure 6.1 *Elements placed into four corners with absolute positioning.*

```
div {
    position: relative;
    width: 150px;
    border: 1px dotted #999;
}
div div {
    position: absolute;
    width: 25px;
    height: 25px;
    background-color: #ccc;
    border: none;
    text-align: center;
}
```

```
div .corner1 {
    top: 0;
    left: 0;
}
div .corner2 {
    top: 0;
    right: 0;
}
div .corner3 {
    bottom: 0;
    right: 0;
    background-color: #999;
}
div .corner4 {
    bottom: 0;
    left: 0;
    background-color: #999;
}
<div>
    Here is some content before the four child div elements.
    <div class="corner1">1</div>
    <div class="corner2">2</div>
    <div class="corner3">3</div>
    <div class="corner4">4</div>
    Here is some content after the four child div elements.
</div>
```

When content is pulled out of the normal document flow, the height of the parent element shrinks. It is easy to run into cases where the parent shrinks too much and the positioned element overflows its parent container. You can force the space open with height, width, or padding on the parent element, as I have done in Figure 6.1. The document, being the root container, will similarly shrink, and you could potentially overflow your document and its scrollable area.

If the containing element isn't forced open—in this case by width on the wide side and other content keeping it open in the vertical side—then the parent container would collapse. If the content were shorter and didn't keep the box open enough, what you might see is shown in **Figure 6.2**.

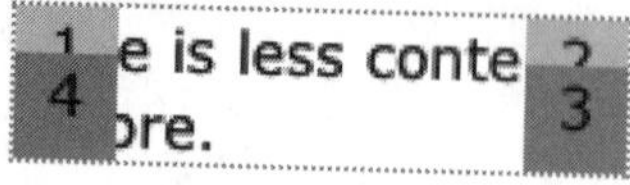

Figure 6.2
A container element shrinking to fit only the content in the normal document flow.

Absolute positioning is the most used method of positioning an element (besides the default value of `static`) and is frequently used in animation; however, it isn't used for many methods of creating layout grids because it doesn't hold that scrollable area open like other methods do.

`fixed`

Fixed positioning is based on the viewport and not the document. The origin for fixed-positioned elements is the root node (`<html>`). The top-left position of 0, 0 would be the top-left corner of the viewport, and similarly the bottom-right position of 0, 0 is the bottom-right corner.

As the name implies, fixed-positioned elements do not scroll with the rest of a document. Because window and viewport sizes typically vary widely (unless you're developing for a specific device or platform such as the Apple iPhone), fixed positioning is most often used for small elements such as toolbars or banners and not for laying out an overall web page.

tip **Fixed-positioned elements are widely supported in current browsers, but if you find you need to support older browsers as well, then you should use a bit of JavaScript code that will position the element absolutely and monitor the use of the scrollbar to change the positioning of the element to keep it in view. This solution can be a little jumpy, so it's best to use `position: fixed` where it is supported.**

Origins and Containing Blocks

Containing blocks and the behavior of managing multiple possible origins for measuring positioning from can be one of the more confusing, but also more powerful, aspects of CSS.

The root element of the document is the initial containing block for which absolute positioning is measured from. However, if any other element is positioned—relatively, absolutely, or fixed in the viewport—it becomes the new origin for its descendant elements. This behavior is probably best illustrated with an example (**Figure 6.3**).

Figure 6.3 *The position of the black* `#innerPositionedBox` *is measured from its containing block.*

```
div {
   border: 1px dotted #000;
   padding: 20px;
}
#containingBlock {
   position: relative;
}
#innerPositionedBox {
   position: absolute;
   top: 0;
   left: 0;
   background-color: #000;
}
[...]
<div id="containingBlock">
   <div>
      <div>
         <div id="innerPositionedBox">
         </div>
      </div>
   </div>
</div>
```

Regardless of how deeply the element `#innerPositionedBox` is nested, the positioning for `top` and `left` is measured from the last positioned ancestor, `#containingBlock`. If you didn't change the CSS code for this example but altered the markup structure slightly so that one of the middle `<div>` elements is `#containingBlock`, then the `#innerPositionedBox` element would instead use that element for its origin (**Figure 6.4**).

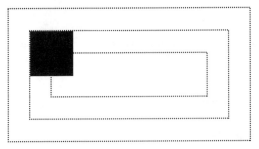

Figure 6.4 *The position of the black* #innerPositionedBox *updated with a new containing block.*

```
<div>
    <div id="containingBlock">
        <div>
            <div id="innerPositionedBox">
            </div>
        </div>
    </div>
</div>
```

Since you cannot escape this behavior and position an element with respect to the root element once it has a different containing block defined, it is important not to overuse positioning properties, thus needlessly creating new containing blocks. Sometimes this is inescapable, and in those cases math can be your friend (either with paper and pencil or in code via JavaScript)—you can calculate the position of the containing block (and any of its containing blocks) and work your way back up to the root element.

z-index

The `z-index` property applies to any positioned box and can be used to control the layering of boxes from back to front. The higher the integer value, the "closer" to the viewer the element appears.

Think of this index as controlling the elements of a stage set in the theater. The background elements are at the 0 position, the actors and other elements may shuffle between 1 and 20, and the foreground set pieces and the curtain are between 21 and 25 (though there is no limit to this value). What happens if two elements in the same stack are at an index of 11 (or 0 or auto)? This isn't a problem unless each element's positioning properties cause them to overlap. In this case, the element specified later in the document flow will appear on top.

This index, like positioning offsets, is relative to the containing block. If one element has a `z-index` of 4 and another element has a `z-index` of 3, none of the second element's children can ever appear "above" the content of the former element.

note **Some plug-in content such as Adobe Flash can sometimes bleed though HTML content positioned above it and given a higher `z-index`. For Flash, in particular, there is a window mode parameter called `wmode` that when set to opaque or transparent will allow content to appear above it in the stack.**

visibility

The `visibility` property determines whether an element renders and can be seen. Unlike setting the `display` property to `none`, an element with a `visibility` of `hidden` still affects layout and will take up space. Unlike the `opacity` property, individual descendants of a `hidden` element can be shown by setting their `visibility` to `visible`.

- `visible`: The element is rendered.
- `hidden`: The element is not rendered.

float

An element with a `float` value of `left` or `right` is taken out of the normal flow of a document and shifted to one side of the containing box. The content that follows it in the document wraps around the floated element's new position.

- `none`: An element is not floated and behaves as normal.
- `left`: An element is taken out of the normal flow and is shifted to the left of where it was to otherwise appear, with content flowing around it on the right side of the element.
- `right`: An element is taken out of the normal flow and is shifted to the left of where it was to otherwise appear, with content flowing around it on the right side of the element.

Think of a small photo that is moved to the right and has text flowing around it; you now have the basic idea of how an element (the photo) behaves when floated (**Figure 6.5** on the next page).

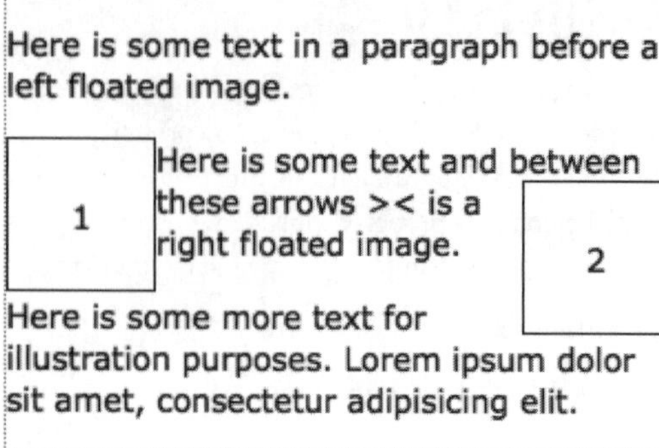

Here is some text in a paragraph before a left floated image.
1
Here is some text and between these arrows >< is a right floated image.
2
Here is some more text for illustration purposes. Lorem ipsum dolor sit amet, consectetur adipisicing elit.

Figure 6.5
Two small elements floated inside text content.

Margins and padding set on a floated element behave as they would on any box in the standard box model and can be used to create a gutter around that element. However, floating has the effect of interrupting the boxes of the wrapping elements leaving their padding, margins, or borders drawn in their normal rectangle, as shown in **Figure 6.6**, rather than moved or redrawn for each individual row of text. Note the way the text touches the right edge of the floated image in this example.

Figure 6.6
Text wrapped around a floated element.

```
img {
   float: left;
}
p {
   border: 5px solid #666;
```

```
    padding: 15px;
    background: #ccc;
}
[...]
<img src="images/1.png" width="67" height="67" alt="1" />
<p>Here is some text after a left floated image for
➥illustration purposes. Lorem ipsum dolor sit amet,
➥consectetur adipisicing elit.</p>
```

Adding a 20-pixel margin around the floated image would create a gutter between the opposite side of the floated element and the content wrapping around it (**Figure 6.7**). After doing this, it is also obvious how the rectangular box drawn by the paragraph including its border and background color are not "wrapping." Only the content inside of those blocks is wrapping.

Figure 6.7
A margin placed on the floated element to create space between it and the content wrapped around it.

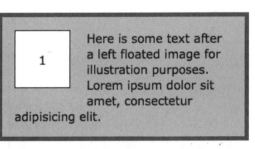

```
img {
    float: left;
    margin: 20px;
}
```

If multiple elements are floated and would appear along the same edge, then they are arranged horizontally with the earliest element in the source appearing closest to the containing block's edge. If the combined width of the floated elements becomes too wide for the containing block's content area, then the later floated elements will wrap. This behaves a bit less like the normal flow of text from line to line and more like how marbles of different sizes will settle as they are placed in a cup. Elements of various sizes are left floated in **Figure 6.8** and right floated in **Figure 6.9** to illustrate the wrapping and ordering behaviors.

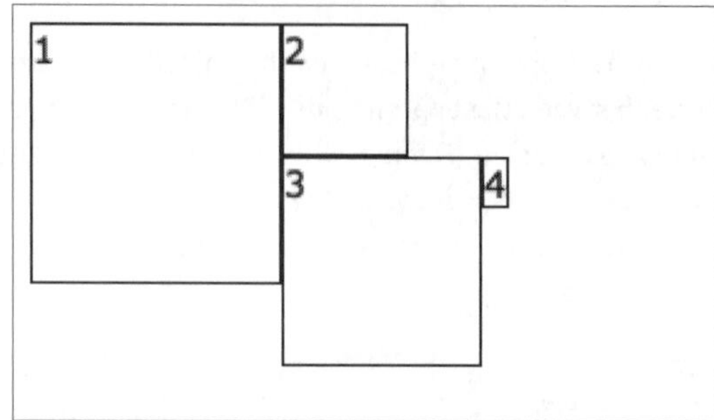

Figure 6.8 *Left-floated blocks of various sizes.*

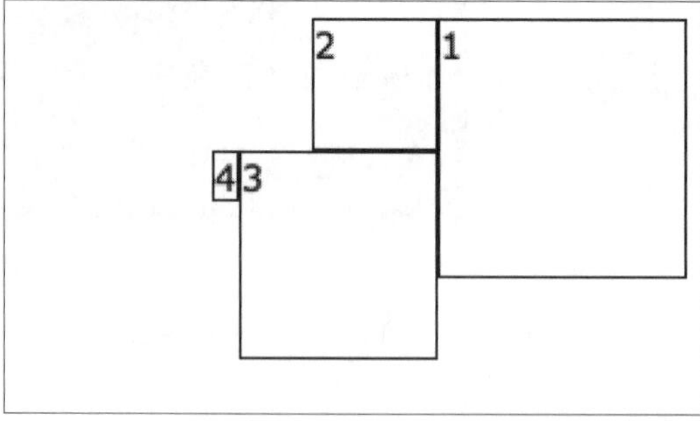

Figure 6.9 *Right-floated blocks of various sizes.*

tip **Floated elements cannot appear before (vertically) elements that come before them in the document, which is why box 4 does not appear next to box 2 even if there were room for it.**

With modern layout techniques, floated elements are used for much more than small bits of content in elements and text wrapping. They can be the basis for placing elements on opposite sides of the same line, controlling a series of tabs, and even controlling multiple-column layout grids.

If an element is positioned with absolute positioning, that positioning will take precedence over the behavior of `float`.

`clear`

Floating is often used instead of positioning or large margins because the content-wrapping effects are desired, but the wrapping of a tall floated element can often extend into later content in an undesirable way. The `clear` property is used to insert a break when encountering a new section of the layout or another unique record in a list or some other reason for wanting to stop the wrapping effect.

- none: The element does not clear any floats.
- `left`: The element will be shifted down to sufficiently clear the bottom edge of any previous left-floated elements.
- `right`: The element will be shifted down to sufficiently clear the bottom edge of any previous right-floated elements.
- `both`: The element will be shifted down to clear and begin after all floated elements.

In **Figure 6.10** you can see what happens when the floated element from one list item bleeds into the following one; things really start to go haywire.

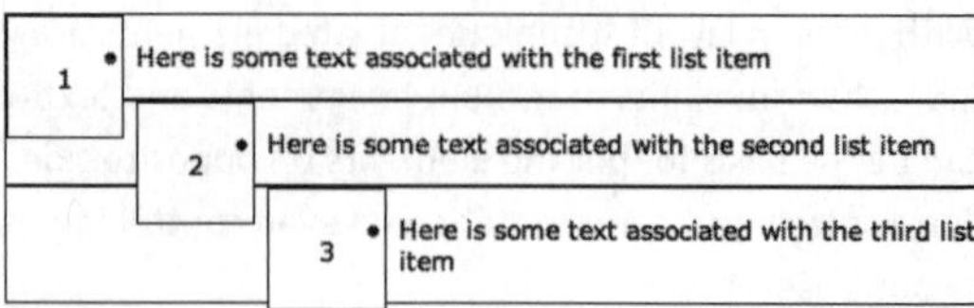

Figure 6.10 *The effect of floated elements extending past its parent element into the following content.*

```
li {
   border: 1px solid #000;
}
img {
   float: left;
   margin-right: 0.5em;
}
[...]
<ul>
   <li>
      <img src="images/1.png" width="67" height="67"
➥alt="1" />
      <p>Here is some text associated with the first list
➥item</p>
   </li>
   <li>
      <img src="images/2.png" width="67" height="67"
➥alt="2" />
      <p>Here is some text associated with the second list
   item</p>
   </li>
```

```
    <li>
        <img src="images/3.png" width="67" height="67"
➥alt="3" />
        <p>Here is some text associated with the third list
➥item</p>
    </li>
</ul>
```

You can set the `clear` property to `left` or `both` on the `<li>` element, as shown in **Figure 6.11**, to make sure that for each new item nothing from the previous item interferes.

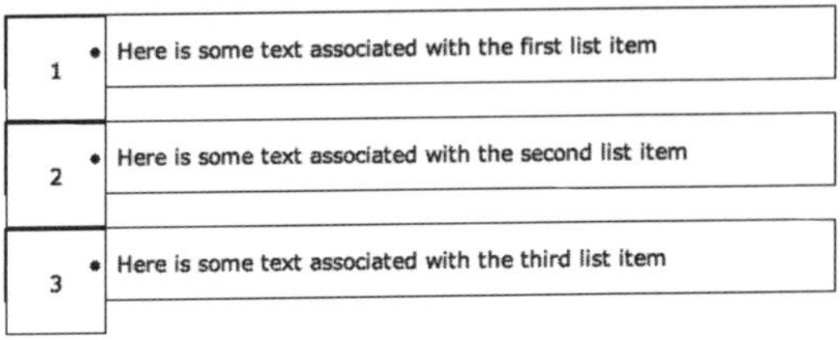

1	• Here is some text associated with the first list item
2	• Here is some text associated with the second list item
3	• Here is some text associated with the third list item

Figure 6.11 `clear:left` *used to stop the previous floats before each new item.*

```
li {
    border: 1px solid #000;
    clear: left;
}
```

tip **The CSS 2.1 Specification has some quite detailed and sometimes difficult-to-understand text explanations of the interaction of floated elements, margins, `padding`, and `clear`. It also has a number of easy-to-understand and useful illustrations (*http://www.w3.org/TR/2009/CR-CSS2-20090908/visuren.html#floats*).**

7 Page Layouts

Page layout with HTML and CSS begins with establishing a layout grid or set of columns to flow content into, but what you do with individual content types or items once you get them into a column is just as important.

Luckily, the techniques used for both page layouts and content layouts are the same. Whether you're working with elements of the content that fall inside each column, content in the page header or footer, or reusable widgets, content elements must be laid out in their own grid using the same techniques that make up the larger page layout.

This chapter introduces the common techniques and building blocks used for laying out HTML content in your pages.

Building Blocks of CSS Layouts

In Chapter 5, through the discussion of the box model and floats, you were introduced to some of the building blocks used to create layouts with CSS. They weren't labeled as such, so what follows is a refresher and a more complete list of building blocks at the core of working with CSS.

Content Is King

As powerful as CSS is, its only purpose is to describe presentation for the underlying HTML content. Strong, semantically appropriate markup is the foundation that allows CSS to work its magic.

Source order, or the order in which content is read when not styled, is also an important consideration when considering which techniques to use to style content. Some techniques may be easier to use to visually pull content from the middle of the document tree or from the beginning or end of a section.

Creating Content Blocks

Chapter 6 introduced the position property and containing blocks.

When styling repeatable content items such as those found in product listings or reusable user profile badges, it is often useful to manage these items as discrete content blocks (or widgets), using `position:relative` to create a distinct, self-referential space in which to work with the individual components of the content item. This widget or block of markup can be placed anywhere in a page and maintain its appearance. **Figure 7.1** demonstrates this effect by creating a user badge in which the user's photo is positioned in relation to the containing block.

Figure 7.1 *Establishing new containing blocks for individual content items and positioning the profile icon.*

```
.badge {
   position: relative;
   width: 155px;
   padding: 5px 5px 5px 72px; /* create gutter */
   font-size: 12px;
   background: #eee;
}
.badge .photo {
   position: absolute;
   top: 5px; /* match padding on .badge */
   left: 5px; /* match padding on .badge */
   border: 1px solid rgb(94,94,94);
}
.badge ul {
   padding-left: 0;
   list-style: none;
}
[...]
<div class="badge vcard">
   <a href="/users/JohnDough" class="fn">John Dough</a>
   <img class="photo" src="images/profile_icon.png">
   <ul class="meta">
      <li>Status: Offline</li>
```

(continues on next page)

```
        <li>Registered: 8/22/2010</li>
        <li>Total Posts: 823742</li>
        <li>Website: <a href="http://example.com/" class="url">
➥ example.com</a></li>
    </ul>
</div>
```

Floating into Margins

Juggling the gutters created by element margins and using the `float` property is at the core of most CSS-based layouts. Although absolute positioning of columns or content items (as was done with the profile photo in the previous example) may seem like the most direct way of placing content side by side, removing content from the document flow or creating new containing blocks can have unwanted side effects.

Instead, floated elements can be moved into gutters created by wide margins on column elements or other content. This layout technique is the basis for the following code, which created **Figure 7.2**.

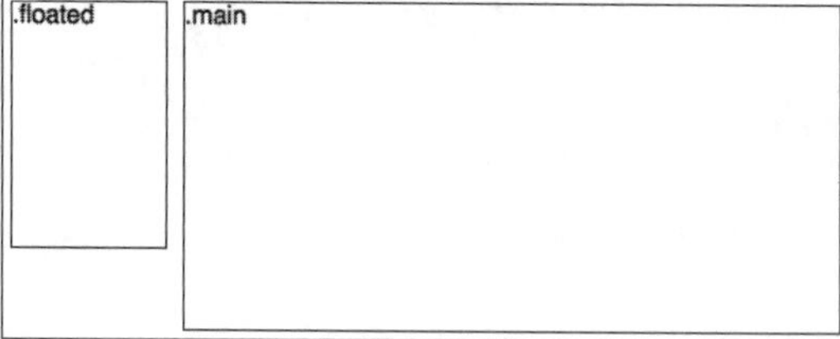

Figure 7.2 *A small content block is positioning in the gutter of a larger element using floats.*

```
.container {
    padding: 5px;
    border: 1px solid black;
}
```

```
.main {
   height: 200px;
   margin-left: 110px;
   border: 1px solid black;
}
.floated {
   float: left;
   height: 150px;
   width: 98px;
   border: 1px solid black;
}
[...]
<div class="container">
   <div class="floated">
      .floated
   </div>
   <div class="main">
      .main
   </div>
</div>
```

This is an extremely common technique when creating multicolumn page layouts, as you'll see in the next section.

Creative Use of Backgrounds

Background images can be more than just repeated background patterns, textures, or fancy border substitutes (Chapter 8). Background images can also be used to create visual structures or separation that doesn't follow the structure defined in the markup.

Faux Columns

In the previous float example, you'll notice that the height of the left element is shorter than the right. If you were to place a background color or image on this element, it wouldn't extend past this element to cover the entire left gutter or column. A background image on the containing element will continue through the whole space, so use that opportunity to apply a background image to provide the appearance of full-height columns. The left column in **Figure 7.3** is an example of this faux column technique.

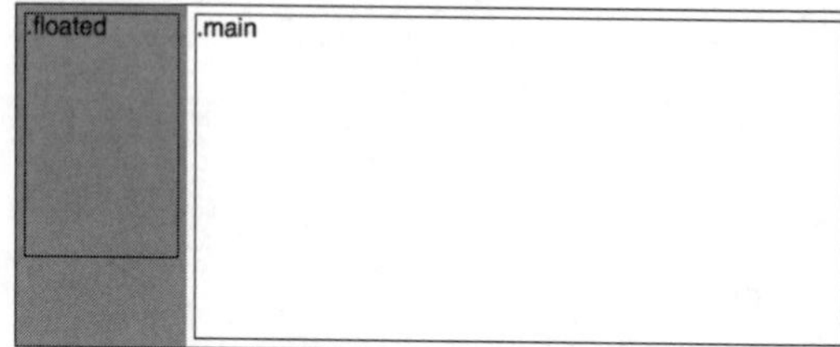

Figure 7.3 *Background image on the container element providing the appearance of a column that extends past the content.*

```
.container {
   padding: 5px;
   border: 1px solid black;
   background: url(images/bg_faux_columns.png) repeat-y left
➥ top;
}
.main {
   height: 200px;
   margin-left: 110px;
   border: 1px solid black;
}
.floated {
   float: left;
   height: 150px;
```

```
    width: 98px;
    border: 1px solid black;
}
[...]
<div class="container">
    <div class="floated">
        .floated
    </div>
    <div class="main">
        .main
    </div>
</div>
```

Background images don't have to be used for clean rectangular columns either. Any parent element right up to the document body is a great hook for applying diagonals, ribbons, waves, or some other graphical appearance that flows between the "physical" boundaries blocks or columns of a page.

Layering Background Images

It is often the case that background images don't cleanly tile or they tile for most of any given direction but then break or shift when interacting with a content element. Imagine implementing a design that has some background elements that repeat horizontally, different ones that repeat vertically, some that don't repeat at all, and one more that repeats in both directions. An inefficient solution would be to make one 10,000 by 10,000 pixel graphic and hope a browser never gets bigger than that.

A more flexible and efficient solution is to deconstruct the background into smaller pieces and then find the element that is best suited to which to apply each background image. The example in **Figure 7.4** (on the next page) uses the `html`, body, and two other elements to overlay four separate graphical pieces.

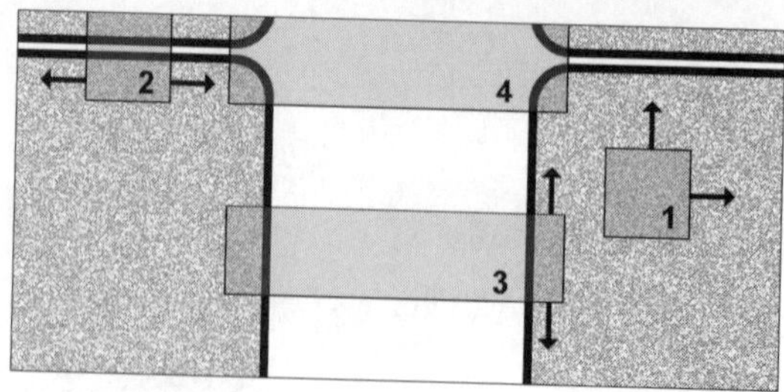

Figure 7.4
A composite of four separate background images working in coordination.

```
html { /* #1 */
   margin: 0; padding: 0;
   background: #fff url(images/fourbg_html.png) repeat;
}
body { /* #2 */
   margin: 0; padding: 0;
   background: url(images/fourbg_body.png) repeat-x left top;
}
.container { /* #3 */
   width: 400px;
   height: 500px;
   margin: 0 auto;
   padding: 0;
   background: url(images/fourbg_container.png) repeat-y left
➥top;
}
.masthead { /* #4 */
   height: 100px;
   background: url(images/fourbg_masthead.png) no-repeat left
➥top;
}
[...]
```

```
<html>
<body>
<div class="container">
   <div class="masthead">
   </div>
</div>
</body>
</html>
```

note **CSS3 includes support for multiple background images on a single element, which provides quite a few more options for layering images. See Chapter 14.**

Inline and Floated List Items

All types of content in a document can be described in lists. Quite often, as is the case for many navigation bars, tabs, and image thumbnails, these structural lists aren't presented as a bulleted list but in a horizontal format. The following code shows a basic example of text-based navigational elements with vertical separators (**Figure 7.5**).

First Page | Second Page | Third Page | Fourth Page | Fifth Page

Figure 7.5 *A set of navigation-based list items floated into a horizontal format.*

```
ul.nav {
   height: 16px;
}
ul.nav li {
   float: left;
   height: 16px;
   padding: 0 0.5em;
   font-size: 12px;
```

(continues on next page)

```
    list-style: none;
    border-left: 2px solid black;
}
ul.nav li:first-child {
    border-left: 0; /* remove border from outside item */
}
[...]
<ul class="nav">
    <li><a href="#">First Page</a></li>
    <li><a href="#">Second Page</a></li>
    [...]
</ul>
```

Using Positioning to Escape Containers

Though the goal of the relatively positioned content blocks described earlier was to create a self-contained area from which to work from, it can be useful to position the parts of those blocks to break out of the four sides of that container. Negative margins were discussed in Chapter 5, but here negative values for positioning are also useful, as demonstrated in the following example (**Figure 7.6**).

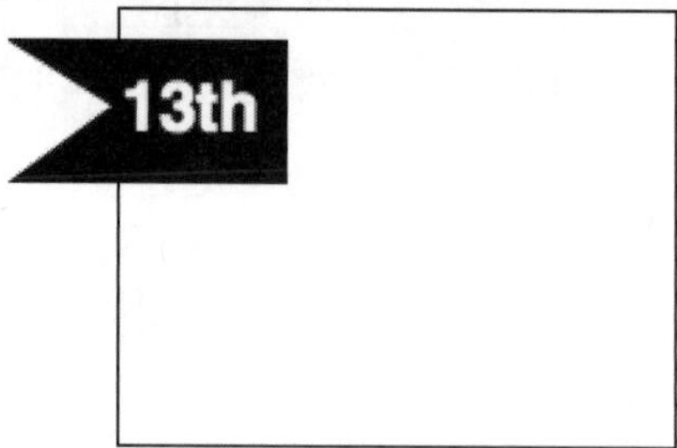

Figure 7.6 *Negatively positioned element breaking its container.*

```
article {
   position: relative;
   [...]
   margin-left: 50px;
   border: 1px solid black;
}
article time {
   position: absolute;
   top: 10px;
   left: -50px;
[...]
   background: url(images/flag.png) no-repeat right top;
}
[...]
<article>
   <time>13th</time>
</article>
```

Overlays, Tooltips, and Drop-Down Menus

Tooltips, drop-down menus, and overlays can be coded in a similar fashion as the example shown earlier in Figure 7.6. The difference with these types of elements is that they typically start as hidden and then through interaction change presentation.

Chapter 14 of *The JavaScript Pocket Guide* by Lenny Burdette (Peachpit, 2010) covers drop-down navigation in depth and includes the following code, which changes the state of the positioned submenu list.

```
#menu li ul {
   position: absolute;
   display: none;
   left: 0;
}
[...]
#menu li:hover ul {
   display: block;
}
```

Hiding Elements: `display` vs. `visibility`

Two ways hiding content can be accomplished are via the two properties `display:none` and `visibility:hidden`. In the case of the `visibility` property, the content continues to occupy the space in the document flow that it would normally. For the `display` property, since the element is no longer a `block`, `inline`, or other type, it is removed from the document flow as if it didn't exist. Unless holding that space open for laying out other elements or maintaining its properties such as `height` and `width` is important for other feature of the page (like in some JavaScript interactions), `display` is typically used.

Multicolumn CSS Layouts

You can use all the tools described in the "Building Blocks of CSS Layouts" section of this chapter for creating the main layout grid for handling the header, footer, and content areas of the page.

The most common approach, because of its flexibility with regard to content lengths, source order, and markup structure, is to use some variation of the "float into margins" technique.

A Two-Column Layout

If you were to make the `.main` and `.floated` blocks earlier in the chapter (Figure 7.3) wide enough, then you have a two-column layout. That isn't all there is to do, however, because that example has two important points of failure:

- If the sidebar column is taller than the main content area, it will escape the bottom bounds of the container and force the wrapping of the following content such as the footer.
- The code provided requires the floated element to appear before the main content area in the source HTML document, which may be undesirable.

Both problems can be solved with minor changes, as the following example demonstrates (**Figure 7.7**).

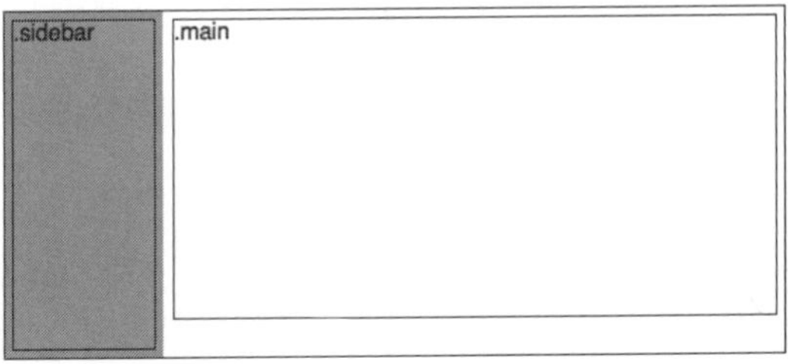

Figure 7.7 *The results of changes to the earlier two-column layout.*

```
.container {
   width: 534px;
   padding: 5px;
   border: 1px solid black;
   background: url(images/bg_faux_columns.png) repeat-y left
➥top;
   overflow: auto;
}
.main {
   float: right;
   height: 200px;
   width: 420px;
   margin-left: 0;
   border: 1px solid black;
}
.sidebar { /* renamed for clarity */
   float: left;
   height: 220px;
   width: 98px;
   border: 1px solid black;
}
[...]
<div class="container">
   <div class="main">
      .main
   </div>
   <div class="sidebar">
      .sidebar
   </div>
</div>
```

Wrapping Floated Columns with `overflow:auto`, `overflow:hidden`, or `.clearfix`

You've seen that when tall floated elements get pulled out of the document flow, their containing element collapses to the height of the remaining content (if there is any). This is often undesirable when that container is intended to be a self-contained content item. There are two ways to prevent this collapsing behavior. You can either hold the container open by clearing the float with a nonfloating content element at the end of the block or force it to grow to include all its contents.

You can accomplish the first by adding additional markup such as `<br style="clear:both">` right before the end of the container. Littering documents with presentation markup should be avoided, and so generated content is often used to emulate this clearing behavior. Full explanations of this technique, often applied by styling a utility class called `clearfix`, is described at Position is Everything (*http://www.positioniseverything.net/easyclearing.html*).

A side effect of setting the `overflow` property on an element to `auto` or `hidden` is that the element should encompass all of its content, regardless of whether that content is floated. In the case of an `auto` height on the container, it will spring back and expand to cover even floated content. This more elegant solution to the float clearing problem, as well as a number of other techniques, is covered in a follow-up to the PIE article by Alex Walker on Sitepoint (*http://www.sitepoint.com/blogs/2005/02/26/simple-clearing-of-floats/*).

Two Columns with Right Sidebar

You've now seen examples of a two-column layout where the first or second column appears on the left. Creating a sidebar on the right just means putting these pieces together and getting the widths and spacing settled. Don't forget to swap the background image as well! The following code shows changes from the code used in the Figure 7.7 example to place the `.sidebar` element on the right:

```
.container {
    width: 534px;
    padding: 5px;
    border: 1px solid black;
    background: url(images/bg_faux_columns.png) repeat-y right
➥top;
    overflow: auto;
}
.main {
    float: left;
    height: 200px;
    width: 420px;
    margin-left: 0;
    border: 1px solid black;
}
.sidebar {
    float: right;
    height: 220px;
    width: 98px;
    border: 1px solid black;
}
```

A Three-Column Layout

You can easily extend the previous two-column layout to incorporate a margin wide enough to float two of the three columns into. However, the size of the main column or the source order may dictate that a different arrangement is needed. Here is some trickery with floating and negative margins to get small left and right columns and allow the main content area to be first in the document (**Figure 7.8**).

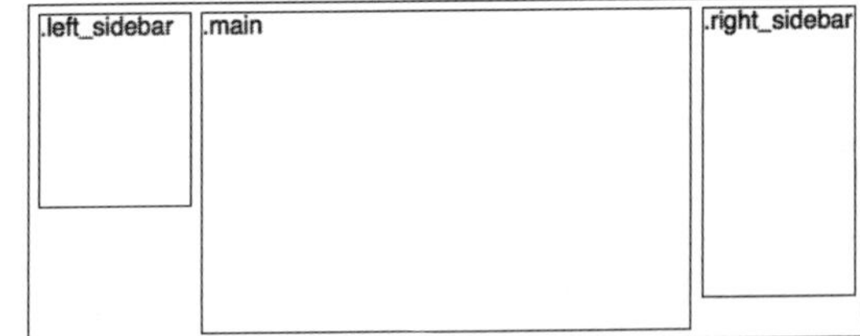

Figure 7.8 *A three-column, fixed-width layout.*

```
.container {
   width: 534px;
   padding: 5px;
   border: 1px solid black;
   background: none;
   overflow: auto;
}
.main {
   float: left;
   height: 200px;
   width: 318px; /* narrower to fit new element and gutter */
   margin-left: 107px; /* make room for left column */
   border: 1px solid black;
}
.left_sidebar { /* renamed, again, for clarity */
   float: left;
```

(continues on next page)

```
    height: 120px;
    width: 98px;
    margin-left: -426px; /* shift _past_ .main */
    border: 1px solid black;
}
.right_sidebar {
    float: right;
    height: 180px;
    width: 98px;
    border: 1px solid black;
}
[...]
<div class="container">
    <div class="main">
        .main
    </div>
    <div class="left_sidebar">
        .left_sidebar
    </div>
    <div class="right_sidebar">
        .right_sidebar
    </div>
</div>
```

tip **A variation of this arrangement and in-depth description can be found in the A List Apart article "Multi-column Layouts Climb Out of the Box" (*http://www.alistapart.com/articles/multicolumnlayouts/*) by Alan Pearce.**

Fixed-Sized, Flexible, and Mixed Columns

The previous layout examples were made with fixed-width columns in a fixed-width container and as a result are called *fixed-width layouts*.

Flexible columns based on percentages are called *liquid layouts* because they flow to fit the dimensions of the browser. Liquid two-column layouts can be just as easily made as their fixed counterparts. Moving to three columns can be a bit trickier, especially when source order considerations dictate the negative margin "jumping" column. This is because percentage margins are calculated relative to the width of the element the margin is applied to, not the containing block's width, so unless the ratios of sizes of each column are simple, it may not be easy to define what "a margin equal to the width of that other element" is.

Mixed-column-based layouts don't have a fancy name, but they consist of both fixed-dimension columns and percentage or autowidth columns. Sometimes these or other complex arrangements are accomplished by nesting sets of containers and columns. **Figure 7.9** and the following code illustrate a fixed-width right column and two additional columns that grow to match the container width.

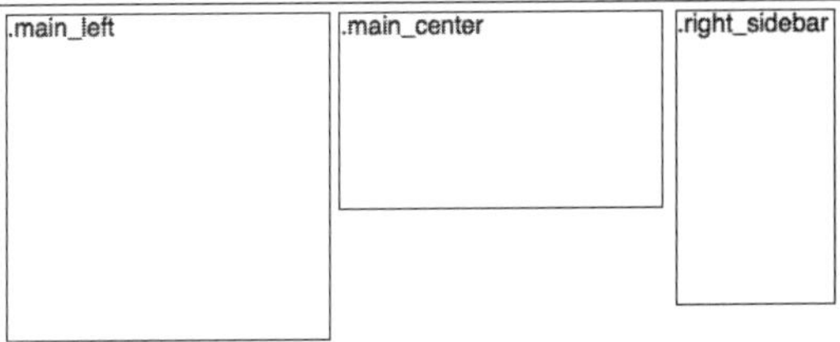

Figure 7.9 *A mixed column layout with two flexible content columns and one fixed-width sidebar.*

```
.container {
  width: auto;
  padding: 5px 107px 5px 5px; /* room for right sidebar */
  border: 1px solid black;
```

(continues on next page)

```
   background: none;
   overflow: auto;
}
.main_left {
   float: left;
   height: 200px;
   width: 48%;
   margin-right: 5px;
   border: 1px solid black;
}
.main_center {
   float: left;
   height: 120px;
   width: 48%;
   border: 1px solid black;
}
.right_sidebar {
   float: right;
   height: 180px;
   width: 100px;
   border: 1px solid black;
   margin-right: -102px;
}
[...]
<div class="container">
   <div class="main_left">
      .main_left
   </div>
   <div class="main_center">
      .main_center
   </div>
```

```
    <div class="right_sidebar">
      .right_sidebar
    </div>
</div>
```

You may be looking at that previous example and thinking that the math doesn't add up, and you'd be right—it doesn't. When mixing percentage measurements, you have to fudge the numbers just a little. A 50 percent width plus another 50 percent width plus 4 pixels worth of borders plus a 5-pixel margin is clearly greater than the 100 percent width that the container has to spare. It is a better bet that 96 percent of that space will leave 9 pixels to spare, which, in this case, will be true so long as the container's content width is at least 225 pixels (9 pixels / (100 percent – 96 percent) * 100). If the content width is larger than 225 pixels, that 4 percent width will be larger than 9 pixels, but in many situations, those few extra pixels are a fair trade-off for having a mixed layout.

Designing with Constraints

Flexible columns are often the best solution for a Web where every visitor has a different screen size and browser size, but that doesn't take into account that the content often has a role to play as well. Content columns that are too small may not fit images or video content, and when they get too wide, the content may be difficult to read. Secondary columns too may have constraints or optimal sizes. Mixed columns can be the best solution.

You can use the `min-width` and `max-width` properties to cap the size of otherwise liquid columns or column wrappers. In the following code, the container used in the previous examples is allowed to grow to between 600 pixels and 1000 pixels and then is centered on the page if it goes beyond the maximum width.

```
.container {
   width: auto;
   min-width: 600px;
   max-width: 1000px;
   margin: 0 auto;
}
```

Chapter 12 covers media queries, which let you match browser or device dimensions (or other properties) with different CSS code. This can be yet another method of introducing a flexible, adaptive layout with constraints.

8

Backgrounds and Borders

Through the color and images of backgrounds and borders, a site's owner or creator can transform bland pages of text into designs that convey a mood, aesthetic, and branding. That is asking a lot of just two seemingly simple properties, but as you'll see throughout this chapter, they're very flexible and powerful properties.

Backgrounds

Backgrounds are an integral part of styling an HTML document. Solid colors, patterns, tiles, gradients, unconventional borders, and nonrectangular shapes can all be achieved by applying the various background properties to the right element.

background-color

The background-color property is applied throughout the content area of the element and is drawn behind any background-image that is set.

- <color>: The color of the background
- transparent: No color fill for the background (default)

background-image

The background-image property is used to specify a background image for an element.

- <uri>: The path to the image file in the format url(path) or quoted with single or double quotes such as url("path") and url('path').
- none: No background image is used (default).

The <uri>, when a relative path, is calculated based on the location of the document containing the given style rule and *not* the source HTML document (unless they are one and the same). This way, you don't have to worry about paths working the same from the HTML documents index.html and /blog/2010/07/27/post-title. It also makes it easier to move the assets together onto a new server or content delivery network.

tip **In most situations, it is suggested you set a background color even if it will be covered by a background image. A slow or bad connection can sometimes mean an image doesn't load or content can become too large for the area covered by a nontiling image. Choose a background color that is sampled from the image or pattern used to maintain the desired readability and visual contrast between the content and the background.**

background-repeat

The tiling of background images is set with the `background-repeat` property. The following keywords are the most commonly used values:

- `repeat`: The image tiles in both directions (default).
- `repeat-x`: The image tiles in the horizontal direction.
- `repeat-y`: The image tiles in the vertical direction.
- `no-repeat`: The image does not repeat.

background-attachment

The `background-attachment` property defines how a background position is determined.

- `scroll`: The background is fixed with respect to the specific element and scrolls along with it in the document. (This is the default.)
- `fixed`: The background is fixed with respect to the viewport and does not scroll with the element; it appears only when that element is "over" its position in the viewport.

background-position

The `background-position` property specifies the position of the background image (or the positioning of the first `background-image` tile when repeating) given as a set of two values: horizontal and then vertical.

- <length>: A fixed length for the offset from the upper-left corner.
- <percentage>: A percentage offset relative to the difference between the size of the container's content area and the size of the image; width is relative to (width of container area minus the width of background-image), resulting in a value of 50% being centered and 100% touching the right edge.
- top: Equivalent of 0% for the vertical position.
- right: Equivalent of 100% for the horizontal position.
- bottom: Equivalent of 100% for the vertical position.
- left: Equivalent of 0% for the horizontal position.
- center: Equivalent to 50% for either position.

A background-position of 0% 0% is the default (the equivalent of left top).

note **When defining the background-position property, it is best to use the same unit type (<length>, <percentage>, <keyword>) for both the horizontal and vertical values. Mixing unit types may yield unpredictable results.**

The CSS3 specification adds the ability to use pairs of values where the first of the pairing describes the edge measured and the second the offset length or percentage from that edge. At the time of this writing, however, no major browsers support the offset syntax.

```
background-position: right 50px bottom 10px; /* positioned
   50px from right edge and 10px from bottom edge */
```

background *(Shorthand)*

The background shorthand property allows for assigning the individual background properties (background-color, background-image, background-repeat, background-attachment, background-position) in the same place.

```
background: rgba(45,45,45,0.5); /* transparent dark gray
   color */
background: #fff url(background.jpg) no-repeat; /* top left
   aligned nonrepeating background image against white */
background: url(circle.png) repeat-y center center; /* image
   placed in the center of the container then tiled
   vertically up and down */
```

note **Like other shorthand properties, when individual properties are left out of the shorthand background property, they are set to their initial values. Therefore, background: rgba(45,45,45,0.5) as in the first example in the previous code would remove any previously defined background images. Use background-color to set color while leaving other properties alone.**

Multiple Background Images

CSS3 defines a way to apply multiple background images to a single element. Supported by Firefox 3.6+, IE 9 Preview, Safari, and WebKit mobile, it may not be ready for use on many projects but may be useful in some situations such as targeting Apple devices. Multiple background images are assigned with comma-separated values for the background-image property (with the earliest image appearing closest to the user). After doing so, the other background image–related properties take matching comma-separated values or a single value applying to all images.

```
background-image: url(top.png), url(bottom.png),
➥url(middle.png);
background-repeat: no-repeat, no-repeat, repeat-y;
background-position: center top, center bottom, center center;
```

The previous code would set up nonrepeating top and bottom images with a tiled image the height of the element beneath them.

Strategies for Background Images

Background images are the most powerful tools in the web designer's toolbox because they can be used in so many different ways. There is no officially sanctioned correct way to use backgrounds, but with experience, you'll notice a few patterns that emerge and common elements to which you can hook backgrounds.

Backgrounds Bigger Than an Element

If you remember the days of using HTML tables for page layouts, you certainly have sliced up your fair share of images into pieces that fit a specific cell only to reassemble them later.

There is very little reason to slice an image for use in CSS. If it appears as a cohesive graphical element in the source Photoshop document, then it can most likely remain so in the HTML build if you find the right element to which to attach it. A typical HTML document structure has a body, a wrapper for the header, center columns or footer, various sections or articles, and then finally the text. Find the element in that hierarchy that is best suited to which to attach the background image.

Stretching the size of an element with excess padding just to make space for an image is common practice when working with columns or link icons. Overlapping elements with negative margins (Chapter 5) can be a great way to get that background image attached to the header element to bleed into the content of the page.

Custom Bullets and Iconography

Applying a custom bullet to list items can be done via the `list-style-image` property (Chapter 10), but positioning is not as flexible as with `background-image`. By turning off list bullets entirely and extending the content area of the list item via `padding-left`, you can make room to shove a new image into (**Figure 8.1**):

```
ul.big {
   margin: 0;
   padding: 0;
}
ul.big li {
   font-size: 28px;
   margin: 0 0 0.25em;
   padding: 0 0 0 30px; /* image is 23x23, shift left to make
   room */
   background: url(images/big_bullet.png) no-repeat 0 6px;
}
[...]
<ul class="big">
   <li>big item one</li>
   <li>another big item</li>
   <li>see the big bullet</li>
   <li>last item</li>
</ul>
```

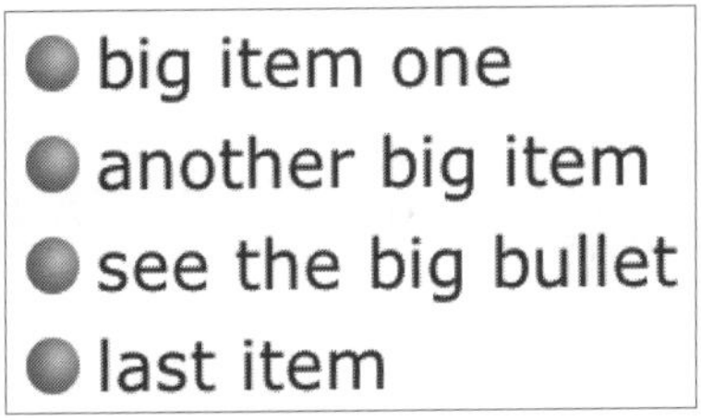

Figure 8.1
Icons placed in gutter created by padding.

The same method is applied for iconography like PDF icons next to links that match the selector `a.pdf` or `a[href~=.pdf]` or warning signs before any `p.note`.

Connecting Backgrounds

Elements such as section headers or tabbed boxes may have fancy borders that "open up" into the content below like the tab on a folder. Because the position of the tab on that folder varies, the opening in the top of the content area needs to change. Here again you can use visual tricks to make the elements backgrounds overlap. The following sample (shown in **Figure 8.2**) uses borders, background colors, and relative positioning to shift the header into the content that follows and create the appearance of a nonrectangular border:

```
h1 {
   position: relative;
   top: 3px; /* shift down the size of the border */
   background: #fff;
   margin: 0 0 0 20%;
   padding-bottom: 3px; /* retain the space of the missing
      border */
   border: 3px solid #999;
   border-bottom: none;
}
h1+p {
   background: #fff;
   margin: 0;
   padding: 1em;
   border: 3px solid #999;
}
[...]
```

```
<h1>Heading</h1>
<p>Lorem ipsum dolor sit amet, consectetur adipisicing elit,
➥ sed do eiusmod tempor incididunt ut labore et dolore magna
➥ aliqua. [...]</p>
```

Heading

Lorem ipsum dolor sit amet, consectetur adipisicing elit, sed do eiusmod tempor incididunt ut labore et dolore magna aliqua. Ut enim ad minim veniam, quis nostrud exercitation ullamco laboris nisi ut aliquip ex ea commodo consequat. Duis aute irure dolor in reprehenderit in voluptate velit esse cillum dolore eu fugiat nulla pariatur. Excepteur sint occaecat cupidatat non proident, sunt in culpa qui officia deserunt mollit anim id est laborum.

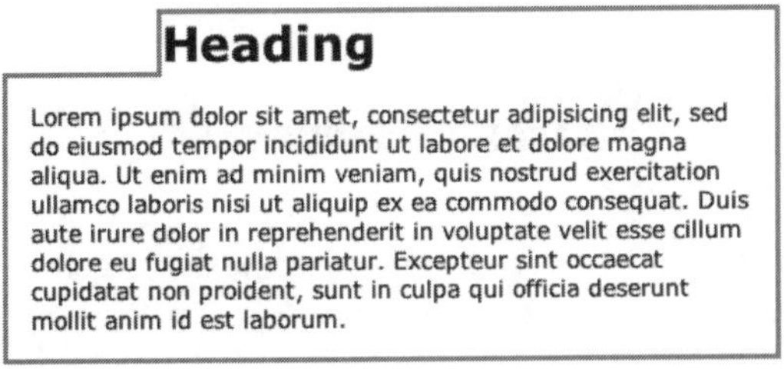

Figure 8.2 *Relative positioning on the heading element, which causes it to appear over the border of the following paragraph.*

Smart Tiling

Whenever using background images with elements that can become quite long on one end or another, such as the height of a content column or the width and height of the body element, there are two options for covering the full length of that block: You can pick a design that can tile, or you can make the image ridiculously big.

The ribbon pictured in the first part of **Figure 8.3** (on the next page) cannot be tiled horizontally as the background image on the <body> element without repeating the dip at some point. Make the image 4000 pixels wide and continue the flat horizontal lines, and you may be confident no one will see the dip again; however, the file size and overhead once the image is loaded will be large.

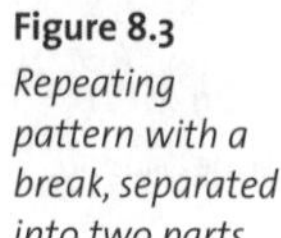

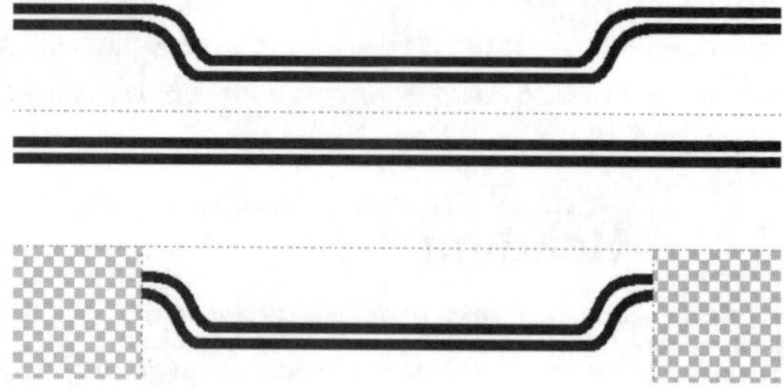

Figure 8.3 *Repeating pattern with a break, separated into two parts.*

Splitting the image into two pieces, one that tiles and one that sits above and covers up the tiling portion, can solve the problem:

```
body {
margin: 0;
padding: 0;
background: #fff url(images/tiled_horizontal_bars.png)
➥repeat-x center top;
}
header {
height: 100px;
width: 400px;
margin: 0 auto; /* center the block */
padding: 0;
background: #fff url(images/the_dip.png) no-repeat center top;
}
```

When working with the background of the document, you have an added challenge that you don't want to extend the content areas unnecessarily and create scrollbars on the viewport. Don't forget that in addition to the <body> element, <html> can also be styled and used as another layer before you have a need for wrapper elements or other artificial hooks.

Cleverness in Web Design

Web design is a craft grounded in the clever use of positioning, margins, padding, borders, and most importantly backgrounds to implement a design of a document or an entire site or application using a very simple vocabulary. Even the table-based layouts of a decade ago were based on the clever cheating of the available tools.

Note the first two column example in Chapter 7 where a background image was used to create the visual appearance of columns even though the image was attached to a single container. The HTML DOM is littered with containers waiting for you to push, pull, and attach images to, so take advantage of them.

Background Image Sprites

The performance impact of having many requests for many different image files used as backgrounds and icons around a web site can be quite large. This can be exaggerated if you have button or icons that have multiple states or you are working with mobile devices where server requests can chew up both bandwidth and battery life. Creating a *sprite* (one image file that contains multiple graphical elements) and then using background positioning to shift the image so that only the desired section of the sprite is visible is a common way to trim down the overhead of these requests.

Take the four different tab "states" shown in **Figure 8.4** placed in the same graphic file.

Figure 8.4
A typical sprite image.

Each section of the image graphic file can be individually applied to a tab by repositioning the file until the desired part of the image is aligned (**Figure 8.5** on the next page).

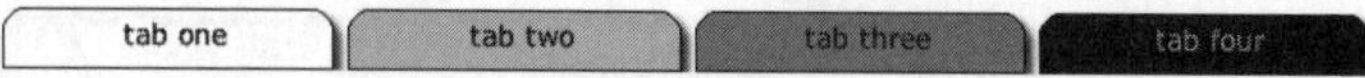

Figure 8.5 *Applying a sprite-based background image.*

```
.tabs .tab {
   float: left;
   width: 177px;
   height: 26px;
   margin: 0;
   padding: 4px 0 0;
   list-style: none;
   text-align: center;
   background: url(images/tabs.png) 0 -31px no-repeat;
}
.tabs .tab.active {
   background-position: 0 -62px;
}
.tabs .tab.special {
   background-position: 0 -93px;
}
.tabs .tab.disabled {
   color: #ccc;
   background-position: 0 0;
}
[...]
<ul class="tabs">
   <li class="tab">tab one</li>
   <li class="tab active">tab two</li>
   <li class="tab special">tab three</li>
   <li class="tab disabled">tab four</li>
</ul>
```

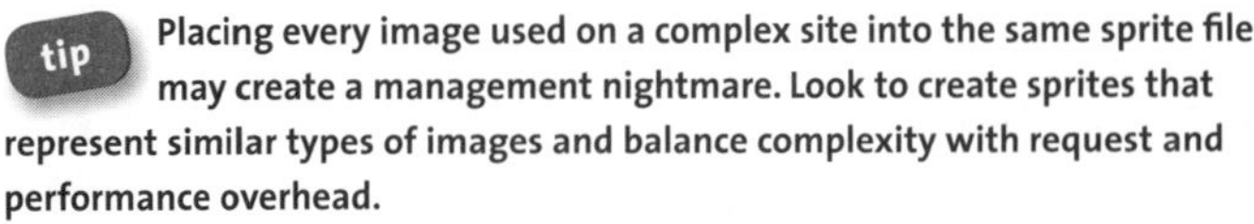

tip **Placing every image used on a complex site into the same sprite file may create a management nightmare. Look to create sprites that represent similar types of images and balance complexity with request and performance overhead.**

Border

In Chapter 5, `border` was introduced as the border on a block element that is drawn between the padding and the margin of an element. Borders are drawn in front of the element's background, which has an impact on the display of border styles with gaps (dashed) and with background positioning.

border-color

The `border-color` property takes one to four `<color>` values signifying the colors for the border on each of a block's four sides. Like with margin and padding, when one color is provided, it applies to all sides. With two, the first value applies to the top and bottom, and the second applies to the right and left. With three, the first applies to the first top; the second applies to the left and right; and the third applies to the bottom. With four values, it applies to each side clockwise from the top. `border-color` can be expanded to `border-top-color`, `border-right-color`, `border-bottom-color`, and `border-left-color`.

border-style

The design of the border is set via one to four keywords assigned to the `border-style` property.

- none: No border drawn
- dotted: A series of "round" dots; roundness varies by browser and border width

- dashed: A series of dashes
- solid: A solid line
- double: Two solid lines separated by a space
- groove: Looks like a groove has been carved by the border
- ridge: Gives the look of a ridge coming out of the canvas
- inset: Gives the appearance that the content was inset into the page
- outset: Gives the appearance that the content was raised from the page

For dotted, double, groove, ridge, inset, and outset, a small border-width value may alter the desired appearance—you cannot round a single pixel dot or find the room within two pixels to draw the two lines and a gap of a double border.

Like border-color, border-style can be expanded into four border-*-style properties.

border-width

The size of the border for each side. See Chapter 5.

border *(Shorthand)*

The border shorthand property accepts up to three values representing border-width, border-style, and border-color.

Additional shorthand properties are available for the individual sides of a block as border-top, border-right, border-bottom, and border-left.

```
fieldset {
   border: 1px solid rgb(100,100,200); /* set all 4 borders */
```

```
    border-bottom: 5px double rgb(100,100,200); /* change
       bottom border only */
}
```

border-radius

border-radius was introduced in CSS3 to allow for rounded corners by providing a radius for the roundness of each corner. Experimental support is included in recent versions of Firefox and Safari by way of vendor extensions and in Opera and the upcoming IE9 directly via the border-radius property. To further complicate things, Firefox has a slightly different order in addressing the individual corners of a block.

The shorthand property border-radius can be expanded (**Figure 8.6** on the next page), as shown here:

```
div {
    width: 250px;
    height: 150px;
    border: 2px solid black;
    -webkit-border-top-left-radius: 30px;
    -webkit-border-top-right-radius: 6px;
    -webkit-border-bottom-right-radius: 30px;
    -webkit-border-bottom-left-radius: 6px;
    -moz-border-radius-topleft: 30px;
    -moz-border-radius-topright: 6px;
    -moz-border-radius-bottomright: 30px;
    -moz-border-radius-bottomleft: 6px;
    border-top-left-radius: 30px;
    border-top-right-radius: 6px;
    border-bottom-right-radius: 30px;
    border-bottom-left-radius: 6px;
}
```

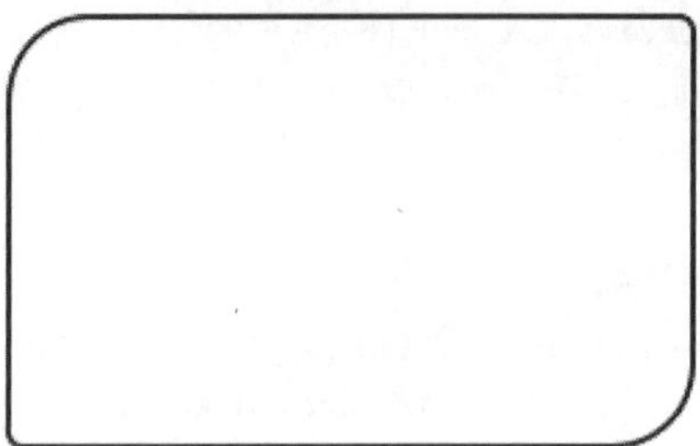

Figure 8.6
`border-radius` *set independently on each corner.*

tip **Web-based tools such as *http://borderradius.com/* provides an interactive tool for setting the border dimensions and generating rules for the various vendor extensions.**

A rounded corner with `border-radius` does not require a border of any dimension. Without a border, the background of the element will still be rounded and cropped. When mixing border styles (**Figure 8.7**) and sizes, browsers will do a best guess to smooth the transitions.

Figure 8.7
Example of mixed border styles.

Outline

Outlines are a special visual property that behave similarly to borders but take up no space in the layout. Outlines are used most often to show focus on a link, active form field, or other element. They can also be useful as a debugging tool—they will highlight an item without shifting its position.

Outline properties are similar to border properties, with the exception that they do not have separate definitions for each of the four sides.

`outline-color`

The color of the outline.

`outline-style`

Uses the same style keywords as border does, with the addition of the keyword `auto`, which is mapped to a device default outline style (or `solid`).

`outline-width`

The width of the outline.

`outline` *(Shorthand)*

The outline shorthand property accepts up to three values representing `outline-width`, `outline-style`, and `outline-color`:

```
:focus {
   outline: 3px auto blue;
}
```

Faking Rounded Corners

The `border-radius` property has growing support with every new browser update, but sometimes design or branding elements are not optional, and you have to find other ways to create the appearance of rounded corners. Clever use of background images can be a way of re-creating the rounded corner look.

This section is not just about re-creating the effects of the `border-radius` property, but it also demonstrates the use of many of the background properties that are used earlier in the chapter.

Required Visual Elements vs. Optional Embellishments

It can be hard to find a strategy for building a site that balances the ease of applying CSS3 effects with the need to make a site look the "same" across web browsers.

If you have the flexibility, break visual element into two groups—those that are important for conveying a site's branding, aesthetic, or emotion, and those that would only reinforce that aesthetic. Then pick your solution accordingly. Rounded corners on sidebars, headers, callouts, and featured elements may be important enough to make it necessary to have them work in the largest number of browsers. Buttons, form elements, thumbnail images, and other content may fall into that other bucket where it would be "nice" to have rounded corners, but if they were squared off, it would be OK, too.

The same goes for other effects such as box shadows or color gradients (Chapter 14), which can be mimicked using background images.

Using a Background Image

With all these great new CSS3 properties being supported, it is easy to over-think and over-engineer solutions to design problems. Particularly when the design requires background images to already be used (so there's no additional bandwidth or maintenance hit), then it may just make sense to create the rounded corner right in the graphic already being used, as in **Figure 8.8**.

Figure 8.8 *One background used to simulate rounded corners.*

```
a.button {
   display: block;
   width: 150px;
   height: 20px;
   padding: 2px 8px;
   text-align: center;
   color: #fff;
   background: #666 url(images/1_part_corner.png) no-repeat;
}
a.button:hover,
a.button:active {
   color: #00f;
}
[...]
<a class="button">fixed size button</a>
```

One Fixed Edge

If a block has one side that is a fixed length but one that expands or contracts based on the space in the layout or the amount of content in it, then rounding all four corners of that box can be faked with just two separate background images, as shown in **Figure 8.9** (on the next page). Usually you can leverage the markup already in the document to attach these two backgrounds to, but sometimes it may require adding a second wrapper element or empty element at the beginning or end to offer the "hook."

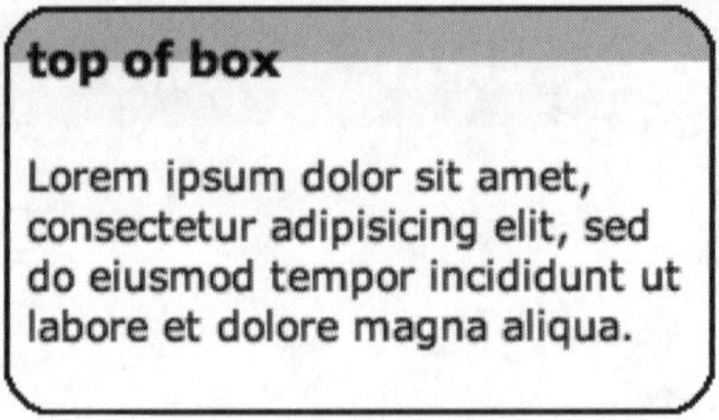

Figure 8.9
Two backgrounds used to simulate rounded corners.

```
div {
   width: 236px;
   padding: 8px;
   background: #fff url(images/2_part_corner_bottom.png)
➥ no-repeat bottom;
}
h3 {
   margin: -8px -8px 0; /* push back out to edge of
      container */
   padding: 8px;
   min-height: 19px;
   background: url(images/2_part_corner_top.png) no-repeat
➥ top;
}
[...]
<div>
   <h3>top of box</h3>
   <p>Lorem ipsum dolor sit amet, consectetur adipisicing
➥ elit, sed do eiusmod tempor incididunt ut labore et dolore
➥ magna aliqua.</p>
</div>
```

This method is quite easy to implement and maintain, and the pattern of having one fixed dimension occurs often in columns, sidebars, and rounded buttons. There are two drawbacks: First the longer (bottom) image can be required to be quite large if it needs cover an unknown amount of content, and second the bottom image can bleed through the outside of the corners of the top element if the outside of the corners is transparent.

note **Why not use multiple background images on one element to do this? The same older browsers that don't support `border-radius` do not support multiple background images.**

Four Corners

In Chapter 6, while learning about absolute positioning, you saw an example (refer to Figure 6.1) that took four small boxes and placed them into each corner of their parent element. You can use this pattern to create hooks to attach background images to, representing each of the four corners. Though this method has more overhead than previous methods and requires some added markup, the results are more flexible than other solutions. **Figure 8.10** combines the four positioned corners with a background image sprite.

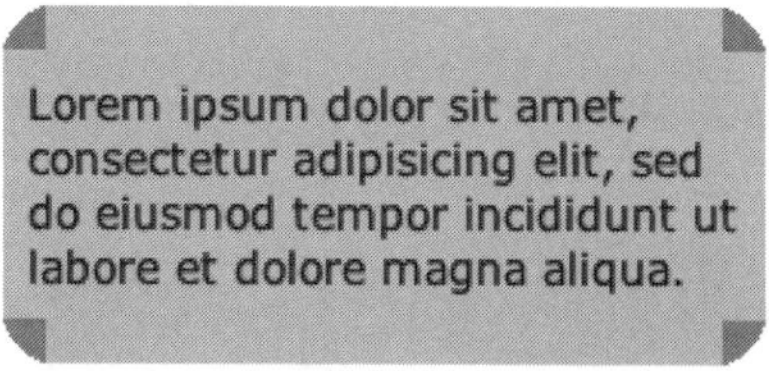

Figure 8.10
Four backgrounds used to simulate rounded corners.

Lorem ipsum dolor sit amet, consectetur adipisicing elit, sed do eiusmod tempor incididunt ut labore et dolore magna aliqua.

```
div {
   position: relative;
   width: 20%;
   padding: 8px;
   background: #CCC;
}
```

(continues on next page)

```
.corner {
   position: absolute;
   padding: 0;
   width: 14px;
   height: 14px;
   background-image: url(images/4_part_corner_sprite.png);
}
.ctl {
   top: 0;
   left: 0;
   background-position: top left;
}
.ctr {
   top: 0;
   right: 0;
   background-position: top right;
}
.cbr {
   bottom: 0;
   right: 0;
   background-position: bottom right;
}
.cbl {
   bottom: 0;
   left: 0;
   background-position: bottom left;
}
[...]
<div>
   <p>Lorem ipsum dolor sit amet, consectetur adipisicing
➥elit, sed do eiusmod tempor incididunt ut labore et dolore
➥magna aliqua.</p>
```

```
    <div class="corner ctl"></div>
    <div class="corner ctr"></div>
    <div class="corner cbr"></div>
    <div class="corner cbl"></div>
</div>
```

tip **Using JavaScript to add these four corner elements into the HTML DOM on the fly is a useful way to keep presentational elements out of your markup and keep your code lean, especially if you are rounding multiple different blocks on a page.**

Drawing Pixels

Taking the positioning of empty elements to an extreme, you can create 1x1 boxes and meticulously re-create the pixels that draw the corners of a containing block. This can allow for visual tricks such as anti-aliasing and changing border radius without having to re-create background image files, but it also makes for lots of code and markup overhead.

Like with the earlier four corners solution, you can use JavaScript to create, plot, and position these extra elements, giving them proper `background-color`. An example of this method is implemented in the Curvy Corners JavaScript library (*http://www.curvycorners.net/*), which uses the `border-radius` property in the CSS document to draw in the rounded corner when loaded in a browser that doesn't already support `border-radius`.

Border and Background Enhancements

Beyond multiple background images and rounded corners, CSS3 has a few other tricks in store that will quickly find their way into web developers' toolboxes. Creating color gradients for background without the use of images and creating borders with images are both covered in Chapter 14.

9

Typography and Web Fonts

In times past, choosing type styling for a web site meant picking from one of a handful of typefaces; setting a size, color, and a few other properties; and relinquishing the control that designers are used to when designing for other media. CSS provides more control over font styling and typesetting than many people realize, and in the last few years there have been huge advancements in tools, services, and embeddable fonts based on changes in CSS3.

This chapter explores how to choose the font used and discusses the other properties that give you control over the appearance and the readability of the text on the pages you build.

Font Basics

The typeface used for rendering text and its particular characteristics such as size and weight are defined using `font` and its related properties.

font-family

The `font-family` property accepts a comma-separated list of font family names. The first value in the list that is installed on the device used to read the page is the font that will be used to style the text.

```
h1 {
   font-family: "Does Not Exist", Arial, sans-serif;
}
```

In the previous code, the font name would be checked; if the font Does Not Exist is not available, the next font Arial would be looked for, and so on, until the generic family `sans-serif` was matched and used. In some cases, font names vary a bit between Windows and Mac, so both names would be listed, like so:

```
p {
   font-family: "Palatino Linotype", Palatino;  /* Windows
   Version, Mac Version */
}
```

Generic `font-family` keywords have been created to map to a browser- or system-defined font family for the specified category of fonts. The preference dialog boxes for each browser typically allow users to select their preferred font family for some of these categories.

- `serif`: A typeface style typically denoted by flourishes or flared ends on each character; typically Times New Roman

- sans-serif: A typeface design with plain or straight features; typically Arial
- cursive: A cursive or handwriting-like typeface
- monospace: A fixed-width font, commonly used for displaying code or other text where character width is important like ASCII art; typically Courier or Courier New
- fantasy: A highly stylized typeface

See "Specifying Typefaces" later in this chapter for common examples and additional discussion of choosing and defining font families.

font-size

The font-size property controls the size of the text in the element and may be defined as a fixed size or a size relative to the font size of the parent element. Browsers set a default size based on settings in the user preferences, commonly 16px.

- <length>: A length measurement
- <percentage>: A percentage value measured against the computed value of the parent element's font-size
- xx-small | x-small | small | medium | large | x-large | xx-large: Fixed-size values along a browser-defined scale
- larger | smaller: A value relative to the parent element's size; typically representing a step up or down the previous scale (xx-small through xx-large)

Relative and percentage font sizes are based on their parent element's computed font size. The effect of this behavior may be compounded when nesting elements. The following sample (**Figure 9.1** on the next page) demonstrates how font sizes are calculated for nested elements.

```
body {
   font-size: 96px;
}
li {
   font-size: 0.5em;
}
[...]
<body>body: 96px
<ul>
   <li>li: 0.5em = 48px
      <ul>
         <li>li: 0.5em = 24px
            <ul>
               <li>li: 0.5em = 12px
               </li>
            </ul>
         </li>
      </ul>
   </li>
</ul>
</body>
```

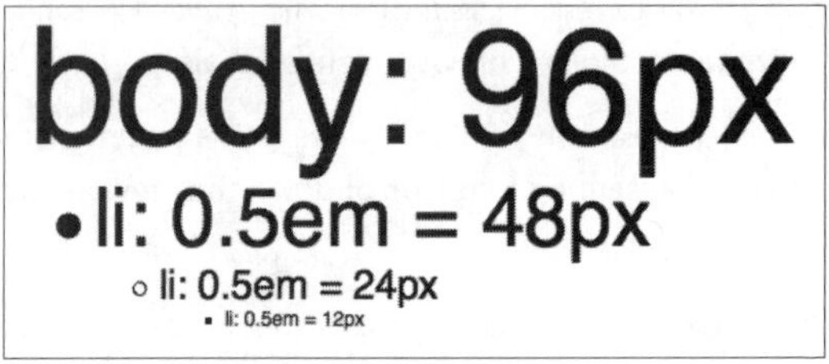

Figure 9.1
Repeated calculation of half the parent's font size.

body: 96px

- li: 0.5em = 48px
  - li: 0.5em = 24px
    - li: 0.5em = 12px

If this compounded calculation of the font size is not the desired behavior, it may be more useful to set the font size on some container element and avoid setting it on list items, paragraphs, or inline elements that may appear in various locations in the HTML document. For the previous example, the following would ensure that all items in the outer container element (`ul`) are half the body size and that this value is not reapplied for nested lists:

```
body > ul  {
font-size: 0.5em;
}
```

note **Many screen-based fonts become difficult to read at small sizes where there may not be enough pixels to distinguish the strokes of a character. Be careful when using relative sizes that make the default font size smaller because some users may have set their default font sizes to something smaller than you're expecting already. Some browsers allow users to set a minimum font size to aid the readability of text to prevent it from becoming illegible.**

Keeping It Relative

There is an eternal debate among web developers about whether it is better (more accessible to those with poor eyesight) to use relative font sizes on a page or whether it is OK to use a fixed-size unit like pixels. Much of the anti-fixed-size argument is centered on the text-zoom behavior of Internet Explorer 6 and older in which the browser will not enlarge fixed-sized fonts.

Even if the base font size you choose is a fixed size (say 12 pixels), it may be worthwhile to use relative units for any individual element-specific or section-specific font size changes. Doing this allows for changing the base font size while maintaining the scale and relative sizes for headers, block quotes, footnotes, and so on, without the need to edit each individual `font-size` property throughout the style sheet.

font-weight

The `font-weight` property controls the weight, or thickness, of the characters in a font.

- `normal` | `bold`: Keywords representing normal weight type (default) and bolded type
- `bolder` | `lighter`: Sets a weight relative to the weight inherited from the parent element
- `100` to `900`: A nine-step scale, in increments of 100, ranging from thin (100) to black (900)

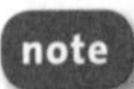

Though a nine-step scale for font weights is defined, browsers typically display only two distinct steps—normal (400) and bold (700).

font-variant

Some typefaces are designed with several variant character sets, including a set of small caps shapes. The `font-variant` allows selection of this alternate set of characters.

- `normal`: Selects the normal variant of a font face (default).
- `small-caps`: Selects the small caps variant of a font face. If none exists, small caps are simulated.

font-style

The style of the font is declared using the `font-style` property.

- `normal`: Normal, upright, type (default).
- `italic`: Italicized type.
- `oblique`: Oblique type. If no oblique style is provided for a typeface, italic may be used.

line-height

The line-height property defines the height of each line of text (line box). Leading, or vertical spacing between each line, is created by specifying a line-height that is larger than the content height (font-size).

- normal: A reasonable default value specified by the browser; commonly 1.2
- <number>: A numeric multiplier applied to the font size to calculate the line-height
- <length>: A specific length value
- <percentage>: A percentage of the element's font-size

font (Shorthand)

The font shorthand property allows for assigning the individual font properties (font-style, font-variant, font-weight, font-size/line-height, font-family) in the same place. Note that although most shorthand properties allow for individual property values to be left out and assume the default or inherited value, at minimum font-size and font-family must be declared. Also, the value of the line-height property must be paired with the font-size value in the format of font-size/line-height, such as 1.2em/1.4.

```
body { font: normal normal normal 20px/1.2em sans-serif; }

/* italic small-caps bold 80px/80px Georgia, serif; */
body>h1 { font: italic small-caps bold 4em/1 Georgia, serif; }

/* normal, normal, 400, 40px/47.3px, Arial, sans-serif */
body>h2 { font: normal 2em Arial, sans-serif; }
```

(continues on next page)

```
/* normal, small-caps, 400, 15px/19px "Trebuchet MS", Verdana,
   sans-serif  */
body>h3 { font: small-caps 15px "Trebuchet MS", Verdana,
➥sans-serif; }

/* oblique, normal, bold, 20px/24px monospace */
body>h5 { font: bold oblique 1em/1.2em monospace; }
```

vertical-align

The `vertical-align` property sets the alignment of text (or other inline content) in relation to the line box controlled via `line-height`. Because this property controls the positioning of an inline element in relation to a line box and not a block element, it is not suitable for aligning block elements in a layout grid. The default value of `baseline` creates an alignment where the bottom of the characters in each inline element on a line all start at the same position. The following are commonly used values for `vertical-align` (**Figure 9.2**):

- `baseline`: Aligns the baseline of the box with the parent element's baseline
- `sub`: Creates a subscript by lowering the baseline of the box
- `super`: Creates a superscript by raising the baseline of the box

```
p {
   font-size: 20px;
   vertical-align: baseline;
   color: #666;
   background: #eee;
}
sup {
   font-size: 1em;
   vertical-align: super;
}
```

```
sub {
   font-size: 1em;
   vertical-align: sub;
}
span {
   font-size: 0.6em;
}

[...]
<p>Baseline xyx <sup>xyx Sup <span>xyx</span></sup> xyx
➥Baseline <span>xyx</span> <sub>xyx Sub <span>xyx</span>
➥</sub> xyx Baseline</p>
```

Baseline xyx xyx Sup xyx xyx Baseline xyx xyx Sub xyx xyx Baseline

Figure 9.2 *Line boxes and vertical alignment with original baseline in black and baselines for sub and super in gray.*

Additional Font Styling

There's more to typography than simply specifying a typeface. CSS provides a rich set of tools for adjusting and customizing the display of text.

`text-decoration`

You can set underlines, strikethrough, or other text decorations (yes, even blink) via the `text-decoration` property. These decorations are drawn separately from borders and are applied only to text.

- `underline`: Each line of text is underlined.
- `overline`: Each line of text has a line drawn above it.

- `line-through`: Each line of text has a line drawn through it.
- `blink`: The text blinks.

tip **Years of conventions have established and reinforced that underlined text signals that the text is a link. Links don't have to be underlined because they may appear as buttons or highlighted via color or background color changes, but if text is underlined, someone will try to click it. I will never say to never do something, but that being said, use `text-decoration: underline` with extreme care.**

text-transform

The `text-transform` property controls the capitalization of text. This can be a useful property for reinforcing the formatting of navigation, buttons, and headers.

- `capitalize`: The first character of each word is forced to be uppercase.
- `uppercase`: All characters are forced to be uppercase.
- `lowercase`: All characters are forced to be lowercase.
- none: No adjustment to the capitalization found in the source HTML document is made (default).

word-spacing

You can adjust the default space between each word in a string of inline text using `word-spacing`.

- `<length>`: A fixed dimension used as an adjustment to the default amount of space between words.
- `normal`: No adjustment is made (equivalent to `0`).

letter-spacing

The `letter-spacing` property controls the spacing of each character in a word. Like `word-spacing`, the `letter-spacing` property defines an adjustment to the default spacing for the font.

- `<length>`: A fixed dimension used as an adjustment to the default amount of space between letters.
- `normal`: No adjustment is made (equivalent to `0`).

text-align

Horizontal alignment of text inside a containing block is defined by the `text-align` property.

- `left`: The text is left aligned (default).
- `right`: The text is right aligned.
- `center`: The lines of text are centered.
- `justify`: The lines of text are flush with both sides of the box, adjusting the spacing in between words as needed.

tip **Be careful when applying `text-align: justify`, particularly with narrow columns. Typographic tools such as hyphenation, which help maintain even character counts per line, are not available to browsers, and they're notoriously awful at calculating the spacing needed for justification. This often results in lines with a few words and huge gaps between them.**

white-space

This property sets how the whitespace and newlines in an element are calculated.

- `normal`: Lines of text are wrapped to fill each successive line box with text; sequences of whitespace (multiple space, tab, or newline characters) are collapsed (default).
- `pre`: Text is considered to be preformatted in the source markup document and whitespace, including newline characters, remains intact (default for `<pre>` element).
- `nowrap`: Whitespace is collapsed as normal, and all text is forced to the same line.

word-wrap

In addition to setting the behavior for `whitespace`, with `word-wrap` you can allow browsers to break lines in the middle of words to prevent long strings of characters from overflowing a box.

- `break-word`: Allows a browser to place a break within a word to prevent a long word with no whitespace characters from overflowing the box; words are broken by character, not syllables, and are not hyphenated.
- `normal`: Single words cannot be broken (default).

text-indent

The `text-indent` property defines an indentation for the first line of text in a block.

- `<length>`: A fixed measurement for the indentation
- `<percentage>`: A percentage length relative to the `width` property of the containing block

text-shadow

- The text-shadow property introduced in CSS3 allows for one or more <shadow> effects to be applied to the text of an element. This shadow is drawn around the letters themselves, rather than around the outer edges of the box like with box-shadow (Chapter 14).
- none: No text shadow is applied.
- <shadow>: A description of a single shadow is <color> <offset-x> <offset-y> <blur-radius> or <offset-x> <offset-y> <blur-radius> <color>, where <blur-radius> is optional and defaults to a length of 0.

```
h2 {
   text-shadow: rgba(0,0,0,0.5) 2px 2px 5px;
/* transparent black shadow shifted right 2 and down 2 with
   a 5px blur */
}
```

You can create the appearance of embossed text by mixing light and dark text-shadow effects, as is done in this multiple-shadow example:

```
h2 {
text-shadow:  rgba(0,0,0,0.3) 0 -1px, rgba(255,255,255,0.3) 0
1px;
}
```

Multiple shadows on the same element are drawn front (first shadow listed) to back (last shadow).

Reviewing Content for Styling and Legibility

When building a site, it is useful to define a base set of styles for common elements to ensure you start off on the right foot with a readable and accessible design based on the chosen font faces, sizes, and colors.

Early in the project timeline there often isn't representative copy written for different page types or content available that includes common tags such as lists, lower-level headings, or text that wraps in uncommon ways. All these elements are crucial to allow for reviewing `line-height`, `text-indent`, or other properties that impact whitespace, aesthetics, and readability. So, how do you code and test the default baseline and ensure you're starting with a readable site if content isn't written and if design comps often have short passages of uniform text?

In 2006 I wrote a blog post outlining the use of a generic test file that contained a wide variety of HTML elements that could be included into the first page you build or could be used in a style guide or inventory document (*http://placenamehere.com/article/178/*). I still use this tag test document for most sites I work on and have placed the code in a project on GitHub (*http://github.com/placenamehere/PNHTagTest*).

Even earlier in the design process Typograph by Iain Lamb (*http://lamb.cc/typograph/*) lets you interact with the style properties of a sample passage of text and experiment with the relationships of type sizes, line heights, whitespace, column widths, and the scale of type.

Both types of tools allow for early adjustment and review of a site's styling and typographic choices and help create a great baseline with which to build the rest of the site elements.

Specifying Typefaces

The choice of font and the availability of font faces can be some of the most challenging aspects of web design. There's a reason that most sites you'll visit appear in Times New Roman, Verdana, or Arial, and that is because there just aren't that many quality fonts installed on enough computers to be reliable options for web designers. Some of that has changed over time, and in the following sections I've outlined a few ways to select typefaces for use on the Web.

System Fonts

Operating systems such as Windows, Mac OS X, Linux, iOS, and Android typically are bundled with a set of preinstalled fonts. Some extremely common applications such as Microsoft Office install additional font files. There are no truly ubiquitous fonts for the Web, because even the most common fonts can be disabled or removed by the computer's owner, but these are some of the most commonly available fonts on desktop browsers:

- Serif typefaces: Times New Roman, Times, Georgia, Palatino Linotype (Palatino on OS X)
- Sans-serif typefaces: Verdana, Arial, Arial Narrow, Arial Black, Helvetica, Impact, Trebuchet MS, Tahoma
- Monospace typefaces: Courier New, Courier, Andale Mono, Lucida Console

To account for a font being unavailable, it is common to list a similar typeface or two before specifying the generic font family, as these examples show:

```
font-family: "Palatino Linotype", Palatino, "Times New Roman",
➥ serif;
font-family: Tahoma, Arial, Helvetica, sans-serif;
font-family: Verdana, Geneva, sans-serif;
font-family: "Andale Mono","Courier New", Courier, monospace;
```

You can find more detailed information on installed fonts in the 24ways article "Increase Your Font Stacks With Font Matrix" by Richard Rutter (*http://24ways.org/2007/increase-your-font-stacks-with-font-matrix*) and on the Code and Style site (*http://www.codestyle.org/css/font-family/index.shtml*).

Font Embedding

To break free of the short list of commonly installed set of "safe" fonts, IE4 introduced font embedding in CSS via the `@font-face` rule. With its standardization by the W3C and more recent adoption by other browser vendors, font embedding is gaining traction, but it is not without the issues that come with early adoption of any technology.

@font-face

The `@font-face` rule allows for defining a custom font family and linking that family to a resource or resources where the font file data resides. Two sets of values are set with this rule:

- `font-family`: The family name for the custom font; used to refer to the `font-family` property later in the style sheet
- `src`: The font source URI and optional (but in practice, suggested) font format

A basic embedded font declaration looks like this:

```
@font-face {
   font-family: "Chris Script";
   src: url(fonts/ChrisScript.ttf);
}
h1 {
   font-family: "Chris Script", cursive;
}
```

If a browser did not support the @font-face rule (or could not find or did not understand the particular format of the font), it would ignore the first font name when it tried to follow the font-family rule for the <h1> element and render the element using the browser-defined cursive font.

A font that may appear on the system can be searched for by font name using one or more local() values before the url(). This prevents the need to download a copy of a font that might be installed on some computers, but it's not ubiquitous enough to be relied on or considered safe for use without embedding.

```
@font-face {
   font-family: "Vera Sans Mono";
   src: local("Bitstream Vera Sans Mono"),
      url(fonts/BSVSM.ttf);
}
h2 {
   font-family: "Vera Sans Mono", "Courier New", cursive;
}
```

If the family name specified in the @font-face rule exists already either by a previous rule or because it is on the user's system, the new definition will take its place.

Font Formats

Like the HTML5 video wars (*http://diveintohtml5.org/video.html*), those attempting to implement embeddable web fonts have to untangle a mess of file format support among the various browsers. And like the video format landscape, browser vendors have chosen to support different font formats because of a mix of licensing and protection issues, platform norms, and legacy behavior. Possible formats include the following:

- `"truetype"`: TrueType fonts (TTF); supported in Safari 3.1+, Chrome 4+, Firefox 3.5+, Opera 10+
- `"opentype"`: OpenType fonts (OTF); supported in Safari 3.1+, Chrome 4+, Firefox 3.5+, Opera 10+
- `"embedded-opentype"`: Embedded Open Type (EOT) embeddable fonts; supported in IE 4+
- `"svg"`: SVG-based font definition; supported in Opera 10+, Mobile Safari
- `"woff"`: Web Open Font Format embeddable fonts (WOFF); supported in Firefox 3.6+, IE 9+

From IE4 to IE8, Microsoft supported only the proprietary EOT format out of concern that embedding TTF or OTF fonts required the raw font files to be posted to a web server for the world to download and because doing so would break the licensing agreements covering most fonts. The WOFF was established in 2010 as a standard format for embeddable fonts that addresses the piracy issues.

Until WOFF is widely supported, to embed custom fonts in IE and the rest of the browsers, you must provide the font in at least two formats and define them similar to the following example.

```
@font-face {
    font-family: "Vera Sans Mono";
    src: url(fonts/BSVSM.eot);
    src: local("Bitstream Vera Sans Mono"),
        url(fonts/BSVSM.ttf) format("truetype");
}
```

For further discussion of offering multiple font format options, see Paul Irish's article "Bulletproof @font-face syntax" (*http://paulirish.com/2009/bulletproof-font-face-implementation-syntax/*).

Creating Embeddable Fonts

So, where do you get all these different font formats if all you have is a TrueType or OpenType font?

The Font Squirrel @font-face Generator (*http://www.fontsquirrel.com/fontface/generator*) takes any uploaded font and converts it into all the formats mentioned earlier as well as offers sample CSS embedding code. Microsoft released the Web Embedding Fonts Tool (WEFT), a Windows utility to create EOT files, and there are WOFF generators being worked on, but since Font Squirrel provides that format as well, individual tools aren't necessary.

Font Licensing and Foundries

Even under the protection provided by the EOT or WOFF format, by distributing a web font, you may be breaking the licensing terms set by the foundry that designed and sold that font. When starting with a fresh design, it may be smarter to start with typefaces whose licensing options are known. Finding good-quality fonts with options for web embedding is getting easier by the day (as I write this, I'm looking forward to the new Fonts.com offerings), with these services among those starting to offer great fonts and tools to legally embed their fonts:

- Typekit: A subscription-based commercial service that works with popular foundries to license and host some of the most popular fonts. *http://typekit.com/*
- FontSpring: Offers commercial `@font-face`-friendly licensing options for the fonts it sells. *http://www.fontspring.com/*
- Font Squirrel: More than just a font file generator, the Font Squirrel site also houses a curated collection of free fonts licensed for use on the Web. *http://www.fontsquirrel.com/fontface*
- Google Font Directory: In conjunction with offering an embeddable API and tool that wraps the `@font-face` declarations as well as providing caching of fonts on its CDN, Google has collected a set of open source fonts, free to use. *https://code.google.com/apis/webfonts/*
- WebFonts.info Directory: As part of a broader wiki devoted to web typography, this is a list of embeddable typefaces and foundries that support embedding. *http://www.webfonts.info/*

Custom Fonts via Text Replacement

Designers can use certain techniques besides relying on system fonts or embedding font files to achieve the look of a custom font. These techniques have pluses and minuses—balancing maintainability, selectability, accessibility, and appearance. They also don't have some of the licensing issues of embedded fonts since font files aren't being shared. Type set inside an image file and placed in the document using an `img` tag is one way to go, but HTML content cannot be changed via a style sheet if a different font is chosen, and the image remains with the HTML source when it appears in other contexts such as RSS feeds.

The font-embedding techniques in the previous section are the new kids on the block and aren't free from implementation issues such as browser support or font licensing, so these older and tested techniques are useful to have in your arsenal.

As with text set directly into an `<img>` tag, these techniques can be useful in small doses such as for article headings or navigation elements, but replacing large blocks of type on the fly provides a good deal of overhead or maintenance problems.

Image Replacement

Rather than use an image tag to display non-HTML-based text, with image replacement, you can use that same image file as a CSS-based background on a more conventional HTML element. After sizing and positioning the background image, the foreground text must be hidden from the user by shifting its position, changing its display value, or doing some similar trick. In the following example (**Figure 9.3** on the next page), headers are presented with the Bitstream Vera Sans font with some embossed effects that cannot be accomplished with CSS- and HTML-based type:

```
h2 {
    display: block;
    height: 25px;
    background-image: url(images/sprite_imagereplace.png);
    background-repeat: no-repeat;
    text-indent: -9999px; /* shift HTML text out of view */
}
#hdrHome {
    width: 80px;
    background-position: 0 0;
}
```

(continues on next page)

```
#hdrBlog {
   width: 63px;
   background-position: -88px 0;
}
#hdrPortfolio {
   width: 107px;
   background-position: -158px 0;
}
#hdrAbout {
   width: 83px;
   background-position: -272px 0;
}
[...]
<h2 id="hdrHome">Home</h2>
<h2 id="hdrBlog">Blog</h2>
<h2 id="hdrPortfolio">Portfolio</h2>
<h2 id="hdrAbout">About</h2>
```

Figure 9.3 *Image replacement for headings.*

Image replacement is a handy tool if used sparingly and for text that will not change often. The technique's major drawback is that it is fairly inflexible and requires images (or an image sprite as in the previous example) to be generated for each piece of text being replaced or edited.

Dave Shea has written a good overview and comparison of some of the code behind various image replacement techniques (*http://mezzoblue.com/tests/revised-image-replacement/*).

Flash Replacement with sIFR

The sIFR project (*http://www.mikeindustries.com/blog/sifr*) uses a Flash object to replace the existing text content and redraw it on the fly in the desired typeface. sIFR uses a two-step process where the browser renders the HTML content based on the styles set in CSS, and then, through JavaScript, a Flash object is created to replace the HTML content. Information on the element its content and its styling are passed to the Flash object, making the system more adaptive when compared to simple image replacement.

The major upside over the image replacement is in the maintenance. A set of images doesn't need to be created each time content is changed, allowing easier use for content such as blog post titles. The major downside is that it does require both JavaScript and Adobe Flash Player (with a fallback to the original styled HTML content).

JavaScript Replacement with Cufón

The Cufón project (*http://wiki.github.com/sorccu/cufon/*) is a toolkit that was built as an alternative to the Flash plug-in sIFR. It replaces the HTML-based type with a non-plug-in-based canvas or VML content instead based on the visitor's browser.

Like sIFR, this requires turning the font into a new format (here, an SVG-based font) and then using a JavaScript-based tool to read in the HTML page as it loads and replace the designated elements with a new rendering component.

10

Lists and Tables

All content types fit into one of two display types—`inline` and `block`. Almost. It may be obvious after thinking about it that tables with their columns, rows, headers, and spanning can't quite be modeled by arranging a series of block elements, but lists with numbering or bullets also need some special tools.

Lists

HTML list elements (`<ul>` and `<ol>`) are simple block elements. Individual list items (`<li>`), too, are sized and positioned with the same box model, with dimensions, padding, margins, and borders behaving as expected. However, each item needs some extra parts to get the markers both positioned properly and designated or incremented properly.

`display: list-item`

The default `display` value for a list item is `list-item`, allowing for the rendering of the box containing the list item marker in addition to the normal `block` behavior for the list item content.

`list-style-type`

You set the type of marker for a list item via the `list-style-type` property. You can use a plethora of keywords as types; they account for everything from the static bullet commonly used for unordered lists to numeric and alphanumeric values for different languages and counting systems. The following are some of the more commonly used types for English-language sites:

- `disc` | `circle` | `square`: Common glyphs; all items in the list will show the same glyph (unless changed explicitly).
- `decimal` | `decimal-leading-zero`: Decimal numbers starting with *1* or *01*, respectively.
- `lower-roman` | `upper-roman`: Lowercase and uppercase roman numerals.
- `lower-latin` | `upper-latin`: Lowercase and uppercase ASCII letters starting with *a* or *A*.
- none: No marker of any kind is rendered.

tip **When setting the `list-style-type` property, don't forget to account for the behavior of nested lists. By default, browsers set different types so that bullets or numbering types change based on nesting helping readability. Set different types for the selector `ul`, the selector `ul ul`, and the selector `ul ul ul`.**

list-style-image

The `list-style-image` property takes a `<uri>` for an image that when specified replaces the generated list marker defined by the `list-style-type` property.

list-style-position

The `list-style-position` property defines where in relation to the list item's box the list marker is positioned. Typically a marker will be positioned outside the content area of the item out into the left gutter; however, it can also be positioned inside of the list item, behaving as an inline element at the beginning of the item would.

- `outside`: The list marker acts an inline element positioned outside the box generated by the item's contents (default).
- `inside`: The list marker is positioned inside the list item's box.

Figure 10.1 demonstrates the two possible `list-style-position` values.

Figure 10.1 *Three list items with markers positioned outside, with the latter three positioned inside.*

- Lorem ipsum dolor sit amet, consectetur adipisicing elit, sed do eiusmod tempor incididunt ut labore et dolore magna aliqua.
- Lorem ipsum dolor sit amet, consectetur adipisicing elit, sed do eiusmod tempor incididunt ut labore et dolore magna aliqua.
- Lorem ipsum dolor sit amet, consectetur adipisicing elit, sed do eiusmod tempor incididunt ut labore et dolore magna aliqua.

• Lorem ipsum dolor sit amet, consectetur adipisicing elit, sed do eiusmod tempor incididunt ut labore et dolore magna aliqua.
• Lorem ipsum dolor sit amet, consectetur adipisicing elit, sed do eiusmod tempor incididunt ut labore et dolore magna aliqua.
• Lorem ipsum dolor sit amet, consectetur adipisicing elit, sed do eiusmod tempor incididunt ut labore et dolore magna aliqua.

Backgrounds as `list-style-image`

A nonrepeating, properly positioned background image on a list item is a common method to give control over precise positioning of list marker images. The following code will achieve this behavior by combining the pattern of using padding to make space for a background image, as shown a few times in Chapter 7, with turning off the default list marker with `list-style-type: none`.

```
ul {
   margin-left: 0;
   padding-left: 0;
}
li {
   margin-left: 0;
   padding-left: 20px;
   list-style-type: none;
   background: url(fancydot.png) no-repeat 4px 4px;
}
```

`list-style` *(Shorthand)*

The `list-style` shorthand property allows for assigning the individual list properties (`list-style-type`, `list-style-position`, `list-style-image`) in the same place.

```
li { list-style: none; }
```

The previous code demonstrates a simple method of disabling markers and shaves a few characters off setting the `list-style-type` property directly.

`::marker` *Pseudo-element*

CSS3 added a handy pseudo-element to access the list marker, both defining and providing a way to change the styles and positioning of the marker that isn't available through shifting or padding on the list item or wrapping the content of a list item in another element, allowing independent control of properties such as `color` and `font-size`:

```
<li><span>list content</span></li>
```

Unfortunately, at the time of this writing, there isn't a browser that supports `::marker`. Combined with counters and generated content, which are discussed in the next section, this will be a powerful way to generate custom markers for content.

Generated Content

As is the case with list markers, it can sometimes be desirable to display content that doesn't come from the HTML document. Generated content is defined with the `content` property and then added to the document as the content of the pseudo-elements `::before` and `::after` (and, eventually, `::marker`).

`content`

The `content` property allows for a number of different types of content that may be added to the selected pseudo-element, including the following:

- `<string>`: Text content for inserting into the element
- `<url>`: A URI of an image
- none: No content is defined

`::before` *and* `::after`

The pseudo-elements `::before` and `::after` represent placeholders for content before and after an element's existing content.

```
a.help::after {
   content: "(?)";
   color: red;
   background: yellow;
}
a.next::after {
   content: url(images/right_arrow.png);
}
[...]
<p>Here is some text that contains a link to the <a class=
➥"help" href="http://example.com/help.html">help page</a>
➥and a link to the <a class="next" href="http://example.com/
➥next.html">next page</a></p>
```

The previous code adds an arrow image after any link to a "next" document and then a question mark after any "help" link, as shown in **Figure 10.2**. These two hints, or similar additions using the content property, are examples of where presentational hints introduced through design would be different from content that would normally be in the HTML source.

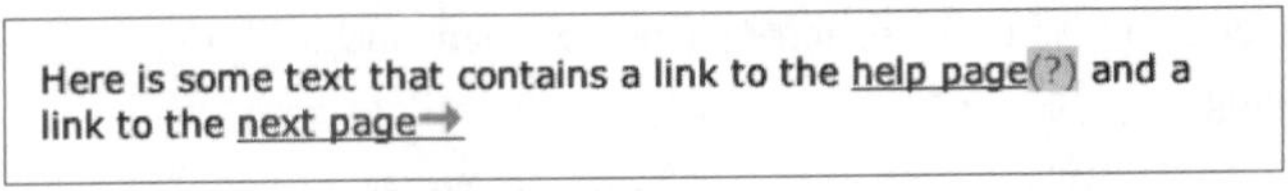

> Here is some text that contains a link to the help page(?) and a link to the next page→

Figure 10.2 *Example of generated content added after links with different class attributes.*

note **The generated content is added to the content of the selected elements. They are styled as though they are content in the original HTML tag, and for links the added content is clickable, just like the rest of the link text is.**

Counters

CSS counters provide the ability to create and use a count of elements of a selected type in a document. Though it would be most useful to aid in customizing item markers, counters aren't limited to lists and can help with document outline style presentations or other embellishments.

counter-increment

The previous specifies that the counter with a provided text label (`<identifier>`) should be incremented when the element defined by the selector is encountered in the document.

- `<identifier>`: The counter to be incremented by 1
- `<identifier> <integer>`: The counter to be incremented and a value (positive or negative) for each step

counter()

Inside the `content` property, the current value of a given counter can be accessed with the `counter()` function:

- `counter(<indentifier>)`: Returns the value of the specified counter
- `counter(<identifier> <list-style-type>)`: Returns the value of the specified counter formatted to fit the provided `list-style-type` value (`decimal`, `upper-roman`, and so on)

counter-reset

- `<identifier>`: Resets the specified counter to 0
- `<identifier> <integer>`: Resets the specified counter to some integer value

The following code was used to generate **Figure 10.3** and demonstrates three presentation options that cannot be accomplished with `list-style-type` in current browsers.

- The list item marker presentation of a number followed by a dot was customized to be a number followed by a colon.
- The text containing the counter can be independently styled from the item content in browsers without `::marker` support.
- A marker and counter was added to each `h4` element.

```
h4 { /* increment one counter at each h4 */
   counter-increment: heading;
}
h4::before {
   content: counter(heading, lower-roman) ": ";
   color: #aaa;
}
ol li { /* start a second counter for list items */
   list-style-type: none;
   counter-increment: item;
}
ol li::before {
   content: counter(item) ": ";
   color: #aaa;
}
ol { /* reset second counter for each new list */
   counter-reset: item;
}
[...]
<h4>Heading</h4>
<h4>Heading</h4>
```

```
<ol>
   <li>list item</li>
   <li>list item
      <ol>
         <li>list item</li>
         <li>list item</li>
         <li>list item</li>
      </ol>
   </li>
   <li>list item</li>
</ol>
<h4>Heading</h4>
<ol>
   <li>list item</li>
   <li>list item</li>
</ol>
<h4>Heading</h4>
```

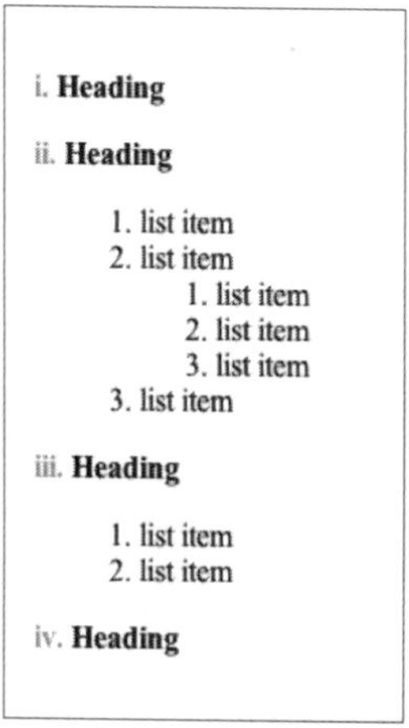

Figure 10.3
Demonstration of counters used for generated content.

i. **Heading**

ii. **Heading**

1. list item
2. list item
   1. list item
   2. list item
   3. list item
3. list item

iii. **Heading**

1. list item
2. list item

iv. **Heading**

Tables

Using tables for creating a layout grid is an outdated web design practice that has generated a lot bad press for the HTML `table` element. Even if that practice has gone the way of the dodo in most modern web development, tables for tabular data are just as important as ever. The layout of a table—with its grid of cells, myriad of borders, and the ability for cells to span rows or columns—calls for some special formatting properties not used for other elements.

The layout model for the table element calls for margins and borders on the outside of the element to behave the same as other blocks and width to be calculated similarly, but it incorporates a few additional properties to control the spacing and display of the containing cells and their padding, spacing, and borders. The following code generates the table shown in **Figure 10.4**:

```
table {
   background: #ccc;
   border: 5px dotted #000;
   border-spacing: 10px;
}
td {
   width: 20px;
   line-height: 20px;
   padding: 10px;
   background: #fff;
   border: 2px solid #000;
}
td[rowspan="2"] {
   border: 10px solid  #666;
}
```

```
tr {
   border-top: 10px solid #aaa;
}
[...]
<table>
   <tr>
      <td> </td> <td> </td> <td> </td>
   </tr>
   <tr>
      <td rowspan="2"> </td> <td colspan="2"> </td>
   </tr>
   <tr>
      <td> </td> <td> </td>
   </tr>
   <tr>
      <td> </td> <td> </td> <td> </td>
   </tr>
</table>
```

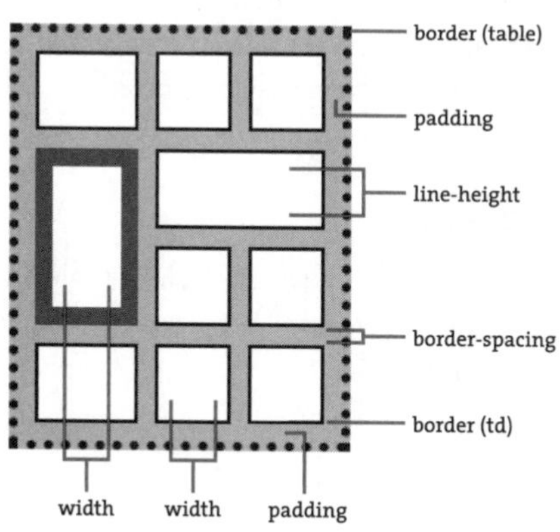

Figure 10.4
A table's layout with `border-collapse` *set to* `separate`*.*

`table-layout`

To maintain the integrity of the grid of cells, the content contained in each cell has traditionally had some impact on the height of rows and width of columns in a table, with the browser free to make adjustments to provided dimensions. Even when a cell width is provided, a large amount of text or a large image may make the cell larger. The `table-layout` property allows for changing the method browsers use to size and render a table.

- `auto`: The width of the table and table cells is established and adjusted as the content of each cell in the table is rendered, with the dimensions provided by the CSS properties and adjusted for size or amount of content (default).
- `fixed`: The width of the table and the table cells do not rely on the content but is determined only by the width of the table and columns, allowing a browser to start rendering the table immediately.

For small tables of data, `table-layout:auto` may be fine, allowing column widths to flex a bit to account for an unexpectedly large number. For much larger tables where you'd want the content to start displaying immediately or for cases where the integrity and uniformity of the cell grid is important, you should use `fixed`.

`border-collapse`

- `separate`: The borders of individual table cells are drawn as distinct features and separated by some border padding. No other parts of a table have borders (default).
- `collapse`: The borders of the table and all parts of a table share the same border on each side.

A few behaviors of separated borders can be seen in Figure 10.4 that make them behave similar to the traditional HTML table rendering:

- In the column on the left, the cells with the narrow border have been adjusted to fit the display of the element with the larger border.
- The border declared on the `tr` element is ignored.
- The table's background is drawn in the spaces between the cell borders.

Figure 10.5 is an example of the previous table with `border-collapse` set to `collapse` and demonstrates the following changes that take place under the collapsing border model that make the table behave more similarly to a typical spreadsheet found in Excel, Numbers, or other software:

- One border is drawn between each cell, rather than a distinct border around each cell.
- Borders may be applied to any of the parts of a table including `thead`, `tbody`, and `tr` elements.
- When elements with different `border-width`, `border-style`, or `border-color` properties touch, they aren't both drawn; instead, one of the styles is chosen by the browser.
- The `border-spacing` property is ignored.

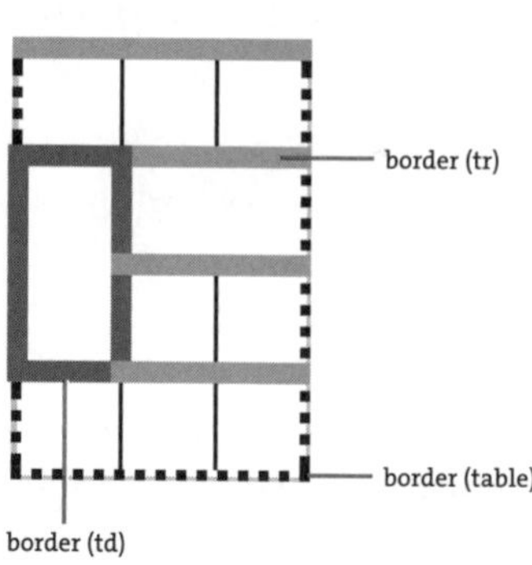

Figure 10.5 *A table's layout with* `border-collapse` *set to* `collapse`.

border-spacing

The `border-spacing` property provides the padding between borders of table cells and takes two `<length>` values, first for the horizontal spacing and second for vertical spacing. If only one `<length>` is provided, it applies to both sides.

empty-cells

In the separated borders model, cells without content (or cells set to `visibility: hidden`) can have their borders and background styling rendered or ignored.

- `show`: Displays the borders and background of an empty cell (default)
- `hide`: Hides the borders and background of an empty cell

vertical-align

Unlike block-level elements, the contents of cells can be vertically positioned inside of the cell.

- `top`: The content of the cell is top aligned.
- `bottom`: The content of the cell is bottom aligned.
- `middle`: The content of the cell is centered in the cell (default).

text-align

The `text-align` property behaves normally when applied to table cells (see Chapter 9).

Table `display` Values

Like the `display` values of `block`, `inline`, and others covered in Chapter 6, non-table-related HTML elements may take on the layout behavior of the various parts of a table. The three basic parts of a table's display are the table, a row, and a cell.

- `table`: A block-level element that generates the outer structure of a table
- `table-row`: A row containing cells
- `table-cell`: An element that represents a table cell

To account for the cases where an element's display property is set to a table-related value but does not have the parent elements that typically make up a complete table structure (table, table row, and table cell), the missing elements may be created virtually. What follows is a sample of the CSS2.1 rules for creating these *anonymous* boxes:

> If the parent P of a "table-cell" box T is not a "table-row," a box corresponding to a "table-row" will be generated between P and T. This box will span all consecutive "table-cell" sibling boxes of T.

Beyond these core three values, there are display values for all the various pieces of a table such as table body, caption, and column groups. The following code illustrates the various table-related values and their context:

```
table { display: table; }
tr { display: table-row; }
thead { display: table-header-group; }
tbody { display: table-row-group; }
tfoot { display: table-footer-group; }
col { display: table-column; }
colgroup { display: table-column-group; }
td, th { display: table-cell; }
caption { display: table-caption; }
```

11

Forms and User Interface Elements

Designing and styling forms and getting constant results across browsers and platforms can be the most difficult part of web development.

Most of this difficulty arises because of the nature of form elements. They're built to solicit input from the user of the site, and how that input gets there can be quite different from device to device.

Different operating systems have different native form control behavior and appearance, and browser vendors have tried to keep the display of interface elements in line with those standards. As a result, a user will typically see familiar inputs even if they use multiple browsers on one device, but if they change devices or operating systems, the interface elements will change. Even in the same browser, the appearances may differ between Windows, Mac OS X, Linux, and mobile devices. **Figure 11.1** shows the difference in appearance of a `select` elements on three different devices.

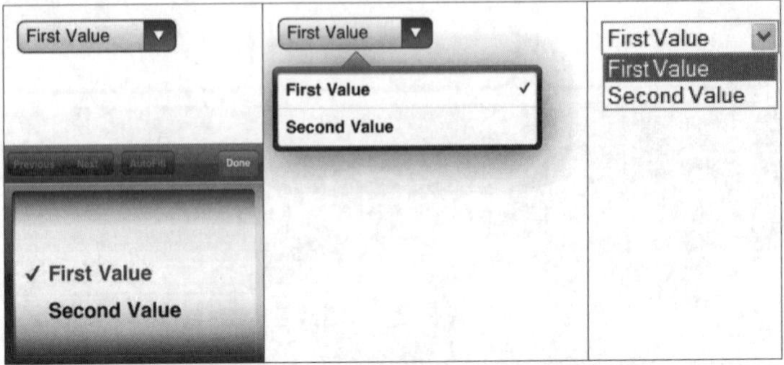

Figure 11.1 *Interaction with* `select` *element in Safari/Apple iPhone iOS4, Safari/Apple iPad iOS3, and IE 8/Windows XP (from left to right).*

You can find additional examples of CSS applied to form elements in different browsers and operating systems at Christopher Schmitt's meticulously collected and indexed collection of screenshots at *http://www.WebFormElements.com*.

Something else that can be unique to form layouts is the need to juggle the myriad of positioning and placement and states of the elements of the form. Large fields, small fields, sets of fields, labels, and help or error messages all need to be placed so that it is clear to the visitor what is being requested from them. The grid that works for a standard-length text input along with its label may not work for a collection of radio buttons or a combination of inputs such as parts of a phone number or city and state.

Working with Form Controls

As different as they can be from platform to platform, form elements on the major desktop browsers tend to share the basic properties; sizing, fonts, colors, and backgrounds all can be set as they would on any other HTML element. Because some form controls are more complex than your average block of text, how those properties are applied can be a bit peculiar. There's no hard and fast rule covering where a border is drawn or what parts of the `select` widget handle a color applied to it.

tip **Safari will draw native form controls (the bubbly look on OS X) even when some styles are defined. Set a border on the element to force it out of the native mode and into one that takes other styles such as color or backgrounds.**

Sizing

Form elements, like images, are inline replaced elements. For styling purposes, it is best to think of them as rectangular boxes even when they're "round" radio buttons or made of multiple parts like file input fields. When setting the height and width of a form element, you're setting the dimensions on the outer box. What the field inside that box does to fill the space is out of your hands.

Although elements such as textareas and buttons fill the entire rectangular box, check boxes, radio buttons (**Figure 11.2** on the next page), and file input fields reserve the specified space in the layout but scale in varied ways to fill that space (or not really *fill* it, as shown in some of these examples).

Figure 11.2 *Radio buttons in Safari 5.0.1/OS X, Firefox 3.6.8/OS X, Firefox 3.0.1.5/Windows, IE 8/Windows, and Opera 10.6.1/Windows (from left to right) with a 100-pixel width, 100-pixel height, 1-pixel red border, and 10-pixel padding.*

To further complicate things, textareas, text inputs, and similar elements aren't quite like the other elements since they follow the content-box box sizing model, whereas other elements use the border-box model. Setting the `box-model` property to `border-box` helps regain some consistency in sizing between text inputs and selects and buttons, with the drawback of making them behave less like the labels or paragraphs that surround the fields.

```
form input[type="text"],
form input[type="password"],
form input[type="file"],
form textarea {
   -ms-box-sizing: border-box;
   -moz-box-sizing: border-box;
   -webkit-box-sizing: border-box;
   box-sizing: border-box;
}
```

Colors, Backgrounds, and Borders

Like sizing, colors apply as you'd expect them to for text in elements such as submit buttons, textareas, and password fields. On the other hand, the behavior of radio buttons, check boxes, and select options will vary based on the browser and platform, so consider the color to be just a suggestion, not a rule.

This goes for the other properties as well. Where would you apply a background color to a radio button—inside the circle or outside and behind the circle in the rest of the box? Is the line between the text space and the little handle of a select element a border? How many backgrounds and borders are there in a file input field that is often represented as something that looks like a text input plus a button? What about all those new input types like sliders in HTML5?

These are the questions that give browser developers (and in turn web developers) migraines.

For the most consistent appearance, you should probably avoid borders and background colors and avoid background images for radio buttons and check boxes. (Figure 11.2 showed examples of browser differences.) On the other hand, you can do interesting things with borders, background colors, and background images for the other field types. In the next example, a background image on a text input is used to create the feeling of depth (**Figure 11.3**). I've added background color change when the element is in focus for a highlight.

```
input[type="text"] {
   padding: 4px;
   width: 100px;
   border: 1px solid #000;
   background: #fff url(images/inner_shadow.png) no-repeat
➥left top;
}
input[type="text"]:focus {
   background-color: #fff335;
}
```

Figure 11.3
A text input with a background image.

Fake It Until Browsers Make It

Clever developers have come up with a whole slew of tricks to get around the lack of styling flexibility with forms in browsers. They get around some of the cross-platform styling quirks inherent in form fields by disabling borders and using fancy background images or using `visibility` and `z-index` tricks, and they get around form styling limitations in browsers by creating complex JavaScript-based interactions. Some methods leave the original input fields intact, but others use JavaScript to replace the standard form input controls and instead use a series of click or other events to control the appearance of nonform fields, storing the resulting values in hidden fields.

Here are a few examples of using CSS and JavaScript to work around form styling limitations:

- Replacing the varied looks of file inputs (see the example at *http://www.quirksmode.org/dom/inputfile.html*).
- Using backgrounds for highly styled radio buttons and check boxes (see the example at *http://www.thecssninja.com/css/custom-inputs-using-css*).
- Implementing new HTML5 input types using custom JavaScript-based widgets such as sliders, date pickers, color pickers, and other types that are part of HTML5 if the visitor's browser doesn't support them (discussed at *http://diveintohtml5.org/forms.html*).

Text and Form Element Inheritance

Stemming from the desire to present native and consistent controls to users, CSS properties that are normally inherited from parent elements to child elements such as font settings and color are not inherited by form elements. Therefore, styling for form elements has to be done by selecting the input field directly. The following code will set the same text color for all the text and form elements:

```
body, input, select, fieldset {
   color: #666;
}
```

Though not supported in IE7 or earlier, this is a great use case for the `inherit` value to explicitly tell form elements to inherit certain properties from their parents.

```
input, select, fieldset {
   color: inherit;
}
```

States: Disabled, Required, and Invalid

Chapter 3 introduced the `:disabled`, `:checked`, `:required`, `:valid`, and `:invalid` pseudo-class selectors. The browser support for these selectors might put them in the unreliable category—particularly since forms are so important to some web apps or marketing programs and thus tend to strive for more cross-browser consistency. These selectors also apply only to form elements and not to other parts of the form presentation like labels that often need to reflect the same state. To get around this limitation, it can be useful to create classes that mimic the effect of the pseudo-class selectors.

```
label.required {
   font-weight: bold;
}
p.errorDetails,
label.invalid,
input.invalid,
```

(continues on next page)

```
input:invalid {
   color: red;
}
input[type="submit"].disabled,
input[type="submit"]:disabled {
   background: #aaa;
   color: #fff;
}
```

JavaScript or server-side form validation can apply these class names to help present the proper state of the elements.

Common Form Element Layouts

By default, labels and forms are inline elements. This is a useful baseline, but creating a form presentation with a clean grid requires some changes to those default behaviors and sometimes a little extra markup or careful use of `fieldset` elements.

Label Stacked Above the Field

Creating a layout where the label is on a line above the form field is as easy as setting the label to display as a block element would (**Figure 11.4**):

```
label {
   display: block;
   margin-top: 1em;
}
[...]
<fieldset>
   <legend>Your Info</legend>
   <label for="fname">First Name:</label>
```

```
    <input type="text" name="fname" id="fname">
    <label for="lname">Last Name:</label>
    <input type="text" name="lname" id="lname">
    <label for="phone1">Phone Number:</label>
    <input type="text" name="phone1" id="phone1" size="3">
    <input type="text" name="phone2" id="phone2" size="3">
    <input type="text" name="phone3" id="phone3" size="4">
</fieldset>
```

Figure 11.4 *Form presentation with labels above form elements.*

Basic Multicolumn Forms

In the previous example, the fields read from the top down. To change the order of elements so they appear from left to right, you can make a small alteration to the styles and markup to give you boxes for elements that float beside each other (**Figure 11.5** on the next page):

```
label {
    display: block;
    margin-top: 1em;
}
div.field {
    float: left;
    width: 50%;
}
[...]
```

(continues on next page)

```
<fieldset>
   <legend>Your Info</legend>
   <div class="field">
   <label for="fname">First Name:</label>
   <input type="text" name="fname" id="fname">
   </div>
   <div class="field">
   <label for="lname">Last Name:</label>
   <input type="text" name="lname" id="lname">
   </div>
   <div class="field">
   <label for="phone1">Phone Number:</label>
   <input type="text" name="phone1" id="phone1" size="3">
   <input type="text" name="phone2" id="phone2" size="3">
   <input type="text" name="phone3" id="phone3" size="4">
   </div>
</fieldset>
```

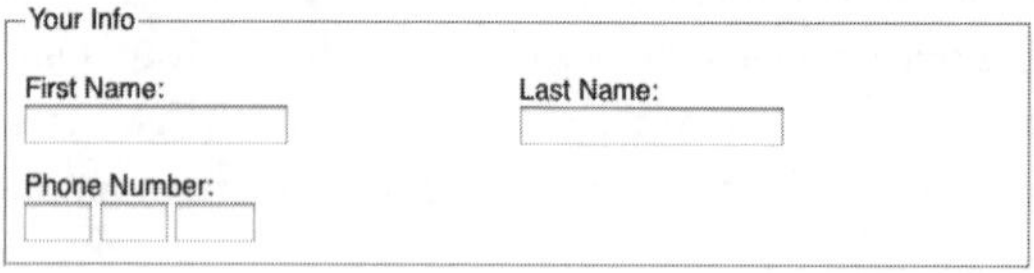

Figure 11.5 *A two-column form layout.*

note **Although including the input field element inside the `label` tag is valid HTML and doing so might allow for easier styling in this scenario, this is considered a bad practice because of accessibility concerns.**

Label Besides the Field

Using the same markup as the previous example and the following CSS, you can have a grid where labels are on the left of the input field (**Figure 11.6**):

```
label {
   float: left;
   clear: left;
   width: 150px;
   margin: 0 10px 0 0;
   padding: 0;
   text-align: right;
}
input {
   margin: 0 0 1em 0;
}
```

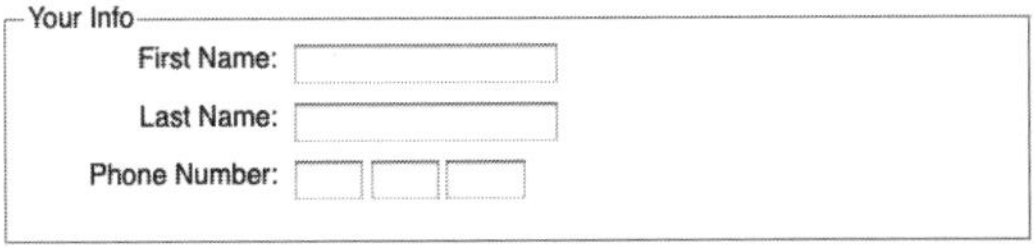

Figure 11.6
Labels to left of form elements.

Exceptions for Radio Buttons and Check Boxes

In the example of the previous label, the form element labels for radio button sets would appear quite awkward with one little small element per line. In the label besides the field example, it may be desirable to have all options on a single line. Or sometimes a check box is associated with a long passage of text such as a legal disclaimer.

The following code builds on the previous examples and demonstrates two possible ways to deal with these exceptions (**Figure 11.7**):

```
label,
span.label {
    float: left;
    clear: left;
    width: 150px;
    min-height: 1em; /* keep empty span open */
    margin: 0 10px 0 0;
    padding: 0;
    text-align: right;
}
[...]
p label,
input[type="radio"]+label { /* reverse baseline label style */
    float: none;
    width: auto;
    margin: 0;
}
[...]
<fieldset>
    <legend>Questionnaire</legend>
    <div class="field">
    <span class="label"></span>
    <input type="radio" name="chooseOption"
➥id="chooseOption[1]" value="1">
    <label for="chooseOption[1]">Option One</label>
    <input type="radio" name="chooseOption"
➥id="chooseOption[2]" value="2">
    <label for="chooseOption[2]">Option Two</label>
```

```
    </div>
    <p>
    <input type="checkbox" name="agree" id="agree">
    <label for="agree">Do you agree to this site's Terms of
➥Service?</label>
    </p>
</fieldset>
```

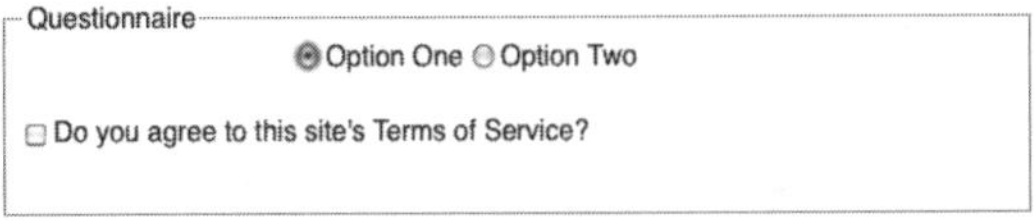

Figure 11.7 *Labels for radio buttons and check boxes.*

Inputting Tabular Data

Though using HTML tables for layout is outdated, taboo, and semantically incorrect, there are arrangements of forms that mimic a table. After all, where is the form data headed most often but a database table or series of tables? So if you have a series of inputs for multiple records at one time or some similar scenario where you can have a one-to-one relationship of data items to cells, marking up the elements as a series of table cells and headers can be semantically appropriate.

Conditional Fields

Sets of conditional fields—if one option is chosen to display or enable other options—typically have states managed by JavaScript, but each state is defined via classes such as the `disabled` class used in the next code block. The script would move the `disabled` class around as the form elements are changed.

```
fieldset.disabled {
    display: none;
```

(continues on next page)

```
}
[...]
<form action="#" method="get">
<div>
   <label for="chooseOption[1]">Option One:</label>
   <input type="radio" name="chooseOption"
➥ id="chooseOption[1]" value="1">
   <fieldset class="extra disabled">
   <label for="option1extra">Extra Info for Option One
➥ </label>
   <textarea name="option1extra" id="option1extra"></textarea>
   </fieldset>
</div>
<div>
   <label for="chooseOption[2]">Option Two:</label>
   <input type="radio" name="chooseOption"
➥ id="chooseOption[2]" value="2" checked="checked">
   <fieldset class="extra">
   <label for="option2extra">Extra Info for Option Two
➥ </label>
   <input type="text" name="option2extra" id="option2extra">
   </fieldset>
</div>
</form>
```

Using a combination of CSS3 selectors, you can achieve similar effects without JavaScript. Using the same markup as the previous example, the CSS would look like this:

```
fieldset.extra {
   display: none;
}
```

```
input[type="radio"]:checked+fieldset.extra {
   display: block;
}
```

Placeholder Text

A fairly common convention with text inputs is to place a small hint into the field. Doing this with the `value` attribute of the element can be problematic (causing the submission of the hint text or other oddities), so HTML5 introduces the `placeholder` attribute. To accomplish this without either attribute, you can create a second label element using JavaScript and position it with CSS over the text input field (as deconstructed in **Figure 11.8**).

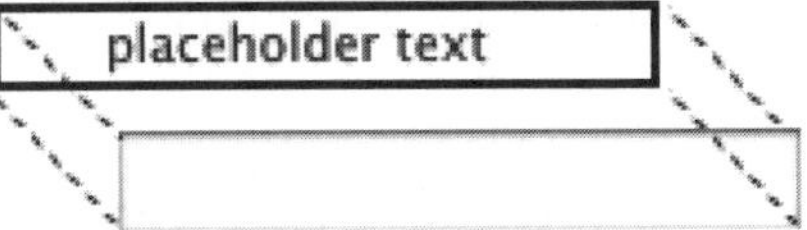

Figure 11.8 *Deconstructing a label covering the input area of a text field.*

Making Buttons

Getting users to interact with a site and share their information is the primary purpose of any form, and for web apps or web-based promotions, clicking the submit button may be the entire reason for the site's existence. As such, submit buttons scream to be styled in ways that draw the user to them. There are 101 different methods to enhance buttons; this section offers a quick overview of the parts behind them.

A key hurdle to easy, flexible button styling is that buttons are just one HTML element, and there is only so much that can be done to one element. You can't manufacture extra hooks for styling like you saw in the rounded corner examples and elsewhere in this book, so you're stuck with what is there (though perhaps you could wrap the button in something or use generated content in interesting ways).

Background Images

Background images can do a lot for a button: add depth, add the look of ready to press and depressed states, and create many other effects that a mix of color and border alone cannot do.

Submit button sizes are typically flexible to allow for a wide range of text lengths or font sizes. A fixed-size button paired with a single nonrepeating background image can lead to text escaping the boundaries of the graphic. With controlled button labels or a large enough button style providing leeway for these cases, the fixed width and height is possible. Otherwise, stick with repeatable patterns and borders used to mark the sides of the element.

CSS3: `text-shadow`, `border-radius`, and Gradients

The `text-shadow` property described in Chapter 9 is a useful way to enhance button text styling. Background images are nice, but they come with some noted inflexibility. The `border-radius` property, when combined with color gradients (Chapter 14), can make creating flexible and good-looking buttons quite simple.

The CSS Tricks Button Maker (*http://css-tricks.com/examples/ButtonMaker/*) is a little demo app that lets you adjust all these properties visually and then shows you the CSS code behind it.

Links As Buttons

Links are often interchangeable with submit buttons in a site's design. The call to action may sometimes be associated with a form but often not. Choose a class to use for links that should be styled similarly to button actions, and style both together in your code. And while you're at it, don't forget the different states for each or the other types of button elements (the `button` element as well as the button `input` type). **Figure 11.9** (on the next page) shows three different clickable HTML elements styled similarly.

```
input[type="submit"],
button,
a.button:link, a.button:visited {
   font: 12px/16px Arial, sans-serif; /* for input */
   padding: 2px 0.5em;
   color: #333;
   background-color: #aaa;
   border: 2px inset #aaa;
   text-decoration: none; /* for link */
}
a.button:link, a.button:visited { /* fix some apparent box
   model differences */
   padding-top: 3px;
   padding-bottom: 3px;
}

input[type="submit"]:hover, input[type="submit"]:focus,
button:hover, button:focus,
a.button:hover, a.button:active {
   color: #000;
   background-color: #999;
}
input[type="submit"]:disabled,
button:disabled,
a.button.disabled {
```

(continues on next page)

```
    color: #fff;
    background-color: #ccc;
    border-color: #ccc;
    border-style: solid;
    cursor: default;
}
[...]
<input type="submit" value="input">
<a class="button" href="#">link</a>
<button>button</button>
<input type="submit" value="input disabled"
disabled="disabled">
<a class="button disabled" href="javascript:void(0)">link
➥disabled</a>
<button disabled="disabled">button</button>
```

Figure 11.9
Links, input buttons, and button elements styled similarly.

12

Media: Printing and Other Devices

CSS is more than a language for describing the presentation of pages viewed on desktop browsers (in this chapter referred to as `screen` media). By specifying a media type associated with a style block, linked style sheet, or group of rules, you can target other media such as print, mobile devices, and screen readers.

Media Types

User agents are categorized by their features, or the features of the device they're running on, into one of several media types. In some cases, such as a desktop browser with a print preview feature, the user agent can support multiple media types; however, only one type will be active at any given time.

List of Media Types

- `all`: Intended for all devices
- `braille`: Intended for Braille tactile feedback devices
- `embossed`: Intended for paged Braille printers
- `handheld`: Intended for small-screen handheld devices
- `print`: Intended for paged, printed media (or print preview)
- `projection`: Intended for projected media
- `screen`: Intended for viewing on desktop and laptop screens
- `speech`: Intended for screen readers
- `tty`: Intended for teletypewriters, terminals, or other devices with a fixed-character grid
- `tv`: Intended for television-based devices with lower resolution and limited scrollability compared to `screen` devices
- Media queries: Intended for a selection of media via expressions that describe the features of the device introduced in CSS3

In practice, your typical web project will have styles targeting the media types `all`, `screen`, `print`, and often `handheld`, while the other types will be left to manage with the styling defined in the `all` type or will be left to the default appearance.

You may find the other types useful in niche projects. For example, if you're designing slides for distribution on the Web after your presentation, then you may have a presentation specifically targeting projected media (which is triggered in Opera's full-screen mode). For more on this idea, as well as information on Opera's support of the `projection` media type, read Till Halbach's article "Creating Presentations/Slideshows with HTML & CSS" at *http://dev.opera.com/articles/view/html-css-slideshows/*.

Specifying Media Types

You can specify the media type associated with a block of CSS rules in three ways: through the `media` attribute on the HTML `<style>` or `<link>` element, as a parameter for the `@import` rule, or as a parameter on the `@media` rule.

`media` *HTML Attribute*

The HTML `<link>` element and the `<style>` element have a `media` attribute that accepts a comma-separated list of media types. The source file linked to or the code in that `<style>` block will be ignored if the device used to visit the page is of a type not listed as one of the values. In the case of the `<link>` element, this means that the linked file may not be downloaded, saving bandwidth.

```
<html>
<head>
<!-- stylesheets for all media -->
<link rel="stylesheet" type="text/css" src="global1.css">
<link rel="stylesheet" type="text/css" media="all"
➥ src="global2.css">
<style type="text/css">[...]</style>
<style type="text/css" media="all">[...]</style>
```

(continues on next page)

```
<!-- stylesheets for print only -->
<link rel="stylesheet" type="text/css" media="print"
➥ src="print.css>
<style type="text/css" media="print">[...]</style>

<!-- stylesheets for mobiles and projectors -->
<link rel="stylesheet" tyle="text/css"
media="handheld, projection" src="compact.css">
<style type="text/css" media="handheld, projection">[...]
➥ </style>
[...]
```

@import *Rule*

Like the designation of media types for link elements, external CSS files included via the `@import` rule can be restricted to specific media types.

```
<style type="text/css">
/* stylesheets for all media */
@import url("global1.css");
@import url("global2.css") all;

/* stylesheets for print only */
@import url("print.css") print;

/* stylesheets for mobiles and projectors */
@import url("compact.css") handheld, projection;
</style>
```

@media *Rule*

The `@media` rule is used to specify that a subset of rules in a block of CSS code should apply only to the supplied media types. As with the `media` attribute of the `<style>` element, any code where `@media` rules are found has already been downloaded. This rule is most useful for targeting devices with small amounts of CSS.

```
/* style rules for all media */
@media all {
    body {
        body: #ddd;
        color: #666;
    }
}

/* style rules for print only */
@media print {
    body {
        body: #fff;
        color: #000;
    }
}

/* style rules for handheld and projection only */
@media handheld, projection {
    body {
        body: #000;
        color: #fff;
    }
}
```

Although you can have an `@import` rule inside a linked style sheet or an `@media` rule inside either type of linked style sheet document, it is not legal to nest an `@media` rule inside another `@media` rule. If you were to define a media type with `@media` or `@import` inside an already restricted block of code, the new media type would further restrict the targeted media list.

Print Media

The printed page, while having many similarities to the screen, differs in many ways as well, most notably that the contents of a document are split across multiple fixed-sized pages rather than one single continuous viewport. The properties listed in this section help control the presentation of each of those pages by offering guidelines about where those page breaks occur within the document's content.

page-break-before and page-break-after

These two properties define whether a page break should occur before or after a given piece of content, which is most useful when applied to articles, headers, tables, or other "blocks" of content.

- `auto`: The user-agent determines the most appropriate places for a page break (default).
- `always`: This tells the user agent to always break before (or after) the selected element.
- `avoid`: This tells the user agent to attempt to avoid breaks before (or after) the selected element.

page-break-inside

The `page-break-inside` property allows for the restriction of page breaks inside a given element's content.

- `auto`: The user agent determines when it is appropriate to place a page break inside an element's content (default).
- `avoid`: This tells the user agent to avoid page breaks within the element's content.

For all the page break properties, the page breaks may be unavoidable, for example when a single element is larger than a single page. The value `avoid` will cause browsers to attempt not to generate a page break, however, and as the name `avoid` implies, it is just an attempt and not an absolute rule.

Browser support for the page break properties is quite mixed, and some browsers have more complete support for individual values than others. You can find a good breakdown and notes on support for the page break–related properties at the Sitepoint CSS Reference (*http://reference.sitepoint.com/css/pagedmedia*) or at the Mozilla Developer Center (*https://developer.mozilla.org/en/CSS_Reference*).

The @page Rule

The `@page` rule exists as a way of setting properties of the page such as margins or orientation. At the time of this writing, the features of `@page` from CSS2 and CSS3 are quite poorly supported (Opera being the one shining star), so it isn't worth presenting the properties in detail.

Print Considerations

The presentation, width, color schemes, navigational elements, and other design features of many web pages may be appropriate for the screen, but not as much when printed. If someone is printing out an article, recipe, or event information from your web site, the last thing they are looking for is half the first page taken up by navigation and advertising and an extra page at the end taken up with nothing but the footer content and repeated navigation links.

To prepare pages for print, a few types of styles are often changed to provide the best printed experience (and not waste your visitor's paper or ink).

- Hide the sidebar, navigation, or other site "meta" elements that are presented on the screen to help when interacting with the site on the screen. Branding elements, logos, and legal information are still important and typically carry through to the print version. Still, be liberal with your use of `display:none`.

- Adjust font sizes, line heights, and other typographic properties to maximize legibility at a typical printed page size.
- Contrast is different in print than on the Web, and backgrounds can make for difficult-to-read pages covered in ink. Hide background images, change background colors to white, and change text colors to the darker shades or even black for the best printing and reading experience.

note **Many browsers will drop background images or similar styles when printing, either by default or by user-selected settings without you explicitly changing them.**

The Print Preview option from your favorite browser will display with any style sheet targeting the print media type and is a great way to test your changes to the print presentation without wasting reams of paper.

Hyperlinks and Generated Content

Printed HTML documents do not display information that may be valuable to the user to have in that printed form. The destination of hyperlinks is one of the pieces of information lost if only viewing the text. Generated content can be used to display the contents of the `href` attribute beside the link text.

```
@media print {
   a:link::after,
   a:visited::after {
      content: " (" attr(href) ") ";
      color: #666;
      font-style: italic;
```

```
    }
}
```

You also might want to consider printing the following: contents of `title` attributes, contents of tabbed boxes, and other content that is initially rendered with `display:none` and meant to be revealed based on user interaction.

Mobile Media

Handheld and mobile devices typically have small physical screens (even as they have increasingly higher resolutions). They also have slightly different interaction models such as touchscreens or heavily keyboard- or tab-based movement.

Mobile Considerations

The smaller screen and slower connection typical of handheld devices are key factors in mobile web development and may drive a "less is more" approach to these devices.

- The slower connection speed and cost of transferring data on some mobile plans can make it desirable to rely more on the default browser style sheet than you would in a `screen` context.
- The touch interface on many smartphones and tablets may drive the need for links and buttons to appear larger, and the spacing between items should be clear to avoid fumbling fingers pressing the wrong item.
- Feature phones, unlike smartphones, offer a limited subset of CSS and a limited layout capability or canvas size. Display and navigation on these devices can also be very linear (left to right, top to bottom), so the positioning and complex element layouts may be ignored.

Though some smartphones have wonderful browsers and deal well navigating conventional web sites, targeting handheld devices with CSS changes alone may not always lead to the best experience for folks because often the types of content or the tasks that mobile visitors are looking for on your site are different from the desktop browser version. Thus, having a separate mobile web site may sometimes be a better option than just feeding the same HTML content with a different set of styles to these visitors.

Media Queries

New in CSS3, media queries add a syntax for describing the characteristics and features of the device being used to view a page, allowing for more precise control or better targeting of those features that might be why you provide one set of styles over another. The following code demonstrates how to target a handheld device in landscape orientation (wider than it is tall):

```
@media handheld and (orientation:landscape) {
   [...]
}
```

The following links to an external CSS file only if the browser (viewport) width is a color device that's wider than 600 pixels, regardless of media type:

```
<link type="text/css" media="color and (min-width: 600px)"
➥ src="default.css">
```

As shown in the previous examples, you can combine media features into a more complex description using the and keyword. You can use the not keyword to negate a media description (or media type) such as in the following example of targeting any nonscreen media type:

```
<link type="text/css" media="not screen" src="alternate.css">
```

The `only` keyword does not logically impact the result of the media query expression; however, it creates a value for the `media` attribute so that browsers that do not support media queries cannot parse into a common media type they support and thus can be used to hide styles from these browsers.

Media Features

The following is a list of media features for which you can specify in a media query expression.

Since the chances that you will have declared the precise viewport width, measured to the pixel (or ems or other `<length>` unit), is quite slim, you can specify the `width` feature as a `min-width` or `max-width`. This holds true of the other features where specified.

- `width`: The width of the viewport or page box; accepts `min-` and `max-` prefixes.
- `height`: The height of the viewport or page box; accepts `min-` and `max-` prefixes.
- `device-width`: The full width of the device screen or printed page; accepts `min-` and `max-` prefixes.
- `device-height`: The full height of the device screen or printed page; accepts `min-` and `max-` prefixes.
- `orientation`: Matches the keyword `landscape` when the width is greater than the height; `portrait` when the height is greater than the width.

- `aspect-ratio`: The aspect ratio of the viewport as described by `width/height`; accepts `min-` and `max-` prefixes.
- `device-aspect-ratio`: The aspect ratio of the device as described by `device-width/device-height`; accepts `min-` and `max-` prefixes.
- `color`: The number of bits of color; `0` for noncolor devices; accepts `min-` and `max-` prefixes.
- `color-index`: The number of individual colors supported by the device; `0` for noncolor devices; accepts `min-` and `max-` prefixes.
- `monochrome`: The number of bits used to describe the monochrome shades available; `0` for nonmonochrome devices; accepts min- and max- prefixes.
- `resolution`: The resolution of the output device measured in `dpi` (dots per inch) or `dpcm` (dots per centimeter); accepts `min-` and `max-` prefixes.
- `scan`: The scan type for television media types; values are `progressive` and `interlace`.
- `grid`: A grid device is a device such as a TTY terminal or a feature phone that has a single fixed-font display.

Responsive Design

In Chapter 7 you learned about building fixed and flexible layout grids as well as setting limits on flexible layouts by using the `min-width` and `max-width` properties. You can use these techniques to make adaptive layouts that find a compromise between the best presentation and readability of the content and the visitor's browser dimensions.

But what if you could adapt the layout from the standard two-column layout into a one-column layout for narrower browsers or bring the footer up into a third column for the insanely wide screens? Or what if you could adjust the size of header type or swap background images so the design feels more proportional to the "page" as presented, while body copy remains at a standard, readable size?

This adaptation of presentation has been dubbed *responsive design*. It takes the standard mechanics of flexible grids, relative sizing of fonts, and other content elements and uses media queries to change the positioning of content, the sizing of elements, or the overall layout grid to respond to the viewport the device is giving you to work with.

For an in-depth review of media queries and how you can use them to design pages that adapt not just to media but also to other browser scenarios, see Ethan Marcotte's article "Responsive Web Design" (*http://www.alistapart.com/articles/responsive-web-design/*).

Browser Support

Media queries are currently supported in Safari 3+, Firefox 3.5+, Opera 7+, Internet Explorer 9+, mobile WebKit, and Opera Mobile. Therefore, there is wide support for them, except for IE 6 through IE 8's large chunk of the desktop market.

It isn't so bad, though, because the support (or lack thereof) can be taken into consideration as just another device criteria in many instances. For mobile development, you're most likely putting handheld device types into two or three buckets already—first specifying the most devices and then breaking smartphones by screen size or orientation. The following example shows a baseline style sheet going to all handhelds and then using media queries with more specific style sheets for those more capable devices:

```
<link type="text/css" media="handheld" src="basic.css">
<link type="text/css" media="handheld and portrait and color"
➥src="enhanced_portrait.css">
<link type="text/css" media="handheld and landscape and color"
➥src="enhanced_landscape.css">
```

You can take the same approach for sites meant for the desktop. Code the base style sheet with the appropriate baseline layout grid, font sizes, and other measurements and serve it to all screen media using the media type declaration. Then use media queries to provide enhancements to those base styles and make a richer or cleaner experience around the edge cases using responsive design patterns.

```
<style type="text/css" media="screen">
/* standard 960px, fixed width two column definition */
[...]
@media (max-width:959px) {
   /* make layout a single column */
   [...]
}
@media (min-width:1200px) {
   /* make layout three columns */
   /* enlarge the font sizes */
   [...]
}
[...]
</style>
```

13

Resets and Frameworks

In the previous chapters, the focus was on understanding the building blocks and elements that make up the language of Cascading Style Sheets. In Chapter 7, we used those elements to create some commonly used layout and grid structures.

But often, the task of building a web site does not start with rebuilding all elements from scratch; instead, it often starts with reusing elements by drawing from a library of code you've previously written or open source code for libraries or elements that you can use.

CSS Resets

In the Chapter 2 discussion of browser- and user-created style sheets, you saw how the default styling for common elements such as paragraphs, links, and forms can be different from each other. Building a site on this inconstant foundation can make cross-browser consistency a more difficult task than it already is.

A CSS *reset* creates a common baseline to work from and zeros out some or all aspects of browser default styling. For example, it is common for browsers to have padding set on the <body> element so that plain HTML content has a little room to breathe. However, it may be easier to style a site if you are instead starting exactly the top-left corner. Font sizes, padding, margin, table properties, and form elements are all typical candidates for being "reset."

Using Resets

It is common to include a reset file so it is the first CSS code that the browser encounters. This is done by inserting its contents into the beginning of the main style sheet for the web site, by referencing it directly using a `<link>` element before your global style sheet, or by using an `@import` statement at the beginning of the main style sheet file, similar to the following:

```
@import url(reset.css);
```

There isn't much to a reset, but a few solid examples have evolved over the years. They're written to normalize inconsistencies between the default setting of various browser or trimming down default rules when they're too overbearing (as in the case of form elements). Whichever one you use, look it over before you use it on a project to make sure it isn't doing anything you don't want (such as setting colors or font sizes).

Eric Meyer's Reset

Eric Meyer's Reset (*http://meyerweb.com/eric/tools/css/reset/index.html*) is widely used and can be found at the core of many larger projects including some of the frameworks discussed later in this chapter.

YUI Library CSS Reset

The YUI Library CSS Reset (*http://developer.yahoo.com/yui/3/cssreset/*) is similar but handles a few properties differently, including applying foreground and background colors. It is available to link to directly from Yahoo!'s servers, which can help with download speed and caching.

HTML5 Reset

The HTML5 Reset from Richard Clark (*http://html5doctor.com/html-5-reset-stylesheet/*) builds on the Eric Meyer's Reset and makes some modifications to sync with new or deprecated elements in the HTML5 specification.

Why Not Reset?

There are two strong arguments against resetting.

Resets can be a blunt instrument. A rule such as `* { margin: 0; padding: 0; }` may have undesirable effects on form elements. On the flip side, explicitly picking a list of elements may mean some elements (old deprecated elements such as `<center>` or new HTML elements such as `<article>`) slip through the cracks.

Not resetting in the first place means not having to re-create common styles like those for emphasis, list indentation, and bullets that were already set by the browser. Also, edge cases or little-used HTML elements (`<dl>`, `<cite>`, `<legend>`) and markup patterns (`<ul>` in a `<blockquote>`) must be tested to make sure that content added to the site later is properly styled.

The type of content appearing on the site will weigh heavily on the appropriateness of a reset. A text-heavy site such as a blog may want to leave more of the browser styling intact, while an application or e-commerce site that relies on smaller content elements may want to be more controlled. Ultimately, the choice to zero out styles at the beginning of a project's code is one of taste and how you prefer to work rather than one of purely technical merit.

Cross-Browser CSS via JavaScript

You can use a CSS reset to create an even starting point for styling individual page elements. But they don't create that same level ground for browsers' support for newer selectors and CSS properties. A drop-in JavaScript *bridge* library may be a convenient way to bridge the gaps in CSS support so that older browsers function like more recent browsers.

When the included library loads, it will typically test the browser's support against a list of CSS features. If a feature is supported, the script will do nothing. However, for those unsupported features, it will comb the style sheet code for their use and then attempt to replicate the behavior of the unsupported CSS through scripting.

You can use JavaScript to check for all CSS 2.1 or CSS3 features missing in a browser, and other libraries are written to target specific gaps in support.

Common Bridge Libraries

There are many JavaScript bridge libraries available to use on your projects, each approaching the task of extending support for the CSS code you've written in different ways.

IE7.js

The goal of IE7.js (*http://code.google.com/p/ie7-js/*) is to make Internet Explorer 5.5 and 6 behave like and support the features of Internet Explorer 7. This includes fixing some HTML and CSS bugs as well as adding support for alpha-transparent PNG images. This may seem like a baby step, but if IE7 is among your target browser matrix and your code is already stable there, you may not need to do more than this to get IE6 in line.

IE8.js and IE9.js scripts are also part of the project, by Dean Edwards, providing similar version bridging support (to match IE8 and IE9, respectively).

Selectivzr

Keith Clark's ie-css3.js (*http://selectivizr.com/*) is an example of a project that aims to add missing selector support (`::first-child`, `::nth-child()`, `[attr]`, and so on) to Internet Explorer 6 through 8. It remains lightweight by leveraging other JavaScript libraries already included in the document, such as jQuery or MooTools, that have selector tools.

eCSStender

Aaron Gustafson's eCSStender (*http://ecsstender.org/*) provides a flexible framework for all browsers for fixing browser bugs or lack of support as well as helping navigate the tangle of vendor extension usage in more modern browsers. Extensions are available that add support for CSS3 features such as transitions, transforms, and `rgba()`/`hsla()` colors in older browsers.

Modernizr

Unlike the previous libraries mentioned, Modernizr (*http://www .modernizr.com/*) does not itself add support for any missing feature or browser bug. Instead, it provides feature detection, the results of which can be referenced from your CSS or JavaScript code. Classes such as `.multiplebgs` or `.no-multiplebgs` are added to the `<html>` element of your document, allowing you to define an alternate set of styles.

More Targeted Solutions

Another class of scripts does not attempt to fix a group of CSS features or fix a specific browser's problems, instead targeting a very specific CSS feature.

The rounded corners discussion in Chapter 8 mentioned using JavaScript to create DOM elements to apply rounded corner effects for browsers that do not support the `border-radius` property. CurvyCorners (*http://www.curvycorners.net/*) is one library that does this for you and is an example of a library that is used to target one specific gap in browser support rather than going after a larger class of problems.

Why Not Use JavaScript?

These JavaScript libraries can be useful to bring a browser in line with the A-grade browsers you're targeting with your CSS code, but they can be overkill. By design, many of these libraries attempt to fix most or all problems with a browser, whereas your project may have only one or two unsupported features or browser bugs that need to be fixed. Why load a script to add support for the `:not()` selector or `border-radius` property if it doesn't appear in your code?

When there are just a few features that would have to be fixed in this manner, it may be more efficient to find alternate ways to code the effects through CSS and HTML rather than turn to scripting. There may be other selectors you can use, for example. In browsers with lower usage, it may be OK just to leave things unsupported.

Likewise, if you are tasked with building a site where you know you have older browsers in that A- or B-grade classification (Chapter 2), you probably will want to avoid some of the unsupported selectors or cutting-edge CSS3 features while building the site. This will ensure that your targets are met and your site displays properly, even without JavaScript enabled, in the largest segment of your user base.

These bridge libraries are best when you have a few noncore elements of the design you'd like to see supported in a wider space or when you're looking to help out the lower-grade browsers that you'd still like to deliver the full experience to.

CSS Frameworks

With so many millions of sites being designed each year, it is a good assumption that any new project that comes along will have a layout grid or other layout properties that may have already been built for another site. Perhaps there are details or contexts of content items that will be unique, but patterns will emerge from the layout grid or other areas that can be transferred from one project to another.

Open source frameworks allow developers to share these patterns and conventions, start with a tested baseline of code, and spend time on the specifics instead of retyping code.

These frameworks include not only a style sheet but also HTML markup patterns and examples for accomplishing common tasks such as a layout grid.

tip **If you're using a popular content management system (CMS), there may be a theme or template that combines a CSS framework with the basic markup and application features already included. The Sandbox theme for WordPress is a good example of this generic baseline with which to work from.**

Common CSS Frameworks

Far from a comprehensive listing, here are a few frameworks that have become popular because of the quality of their code and their flexibility.

Blueprint

Blueprint (*http://www.blueprintcss.org/*) provides a broad starting point for starting to build a site including a reset, layout grid tools, and baseline typographic and form styling. There are also plug-ins or examples for common content elements such as tabs, buttons, and iconography.

960

The 960 grid system (*http://960.gs/*) takes a 960-pixel area and allows you to specify a 12- or 16-column grid with 20-pixel gutters between them. This split, and the code that is generated and provided for you to place content in the grid, allows you to quickly put a page layout together. The sizing and spacing rules offer a very controlled grid to design a site from without being too restrictive.

Object Oriented CSS (OOCSS)

As much code philosophy as framework, Object Oriented CSS (*http://wiki.github.com/stubbornella/oocss/* or *http://oocss.org*), spearheaded by Nicole Sullivan, focuses on content elements first. It breaks down the content into pieces and modules and uses their similarities to define a common language of content labels applied as class names. This is particularly useful for large sites because it takes full advantage of the cascading aspects of CSS to help maintain consistency across the many different content types typical of larger web sites.

YUI Library

The Reset file I mentioned earlier is just a small part of the YUI Library. The larger project is comprised of a baseline set of CSS files , baseline JavaScript files, and components for common web application interface components such as cookie access, drag-and-dropped elements, date pickers, and sliders. Similar interface widget libraries are available from jQuery UI, script.aculo.us, and MochaUI. They all provide a collection of widgets to choose from and rules for embedding and skinning those content elements, but they do not offer the more general reset and framework aspects that YUI does.

Why Not Use a Framework?

Like any other tool, frameworks are developed with certain priorities based on the specific problems developers are attempting to solve. As they evolve, they may become more generic, but each framework maintains these priorities that are sometimes not the same as your needs on any given project.

For instance, the YUI tools tend to be a bit more web application focused, and OOCSS works best when the site is complex enough to have the depth of content types to manage. Attempting to go against the grain will cause you to write more code than what you'd save and will cause you more headaches than starting from scratch.

Beyond Frameworks

Frameworks provide a starting point to begin developing a web site, but they don't change how you write and edit CSS code. All the rules of inheritance, specificity, source order, and syntax discussed in this book continue to apply for any site-specific code you add on top of a chosen framework.

There is an emerging class of tools for authoring and generating CSS code that makes small modifications to the language and allows helpers such as variables and selector nesting to be used. These changes remove some of the repetition and document searching that typically come with building and maintaining styles for a larger site.

CSS Preprocessors

To turn the written code back into code in a syntax, browsers understand a conversion layer (preprocessor) is added as a compilation step via tools on your local development machine or via server-side scripts.

Less

Less (*http://lesscss.org/*) is a Ruby gem that adds the ability to include the CSS rules from one selector into another (a mixin), selector nesting, simple mathematical formulas, and variables that stand in for values so that colors, sizes, and other values need to be typed only once. The following is an example of both a variable definition and a nested rule as written using Less:

```
@highlight_color: #eaa;
blockquote {
    font-size: 1.4em;
    a {
        text-style: italic;
        background-color: @highlight_color;
    }
}
```

The previous code gets compiled into the following final code that gets sent to the visitors' browsers:

```
blockquote {
   font-size: 1.4em;
}
blockquote a {
   text-style: italic;
   background-color: #eaa;
}
```

Sass

Sass (*http://sass-lang.com/*) is also a Ruby gem and offers variable, mixin, math, and nesting features similar to Less. It has two different syntaxes to choose from, one similar to CSS (and Less) and an alternate syntax that breaks from the brackets and colons of CSS into a tab-based style some may find more readable or manageable.

14

The Not Too Distant Future of CSS

As CSS has evolved as a language, it has often attempted to make common tasks that may be difficult or inflexible quite easy. Some of these new properties are based on experimental properties in individual browsers, but often they're based on design and code patterns used every day by developers.

For example, the need to use multiple HTML elements as hooks so that multiple background images can be used (shown in Figure 7.4), and the frequency with which this is done, has led to CSS changes that support multiple background images on a single element, as you saw in Chapter 8.

Several CSS3 features have been covered in previous chapters because they have broad support in modern browsers, they are used to accomplish enhancements without major impact on the design if not supported, or both. Either way, they can be incorporated into the toolbox for most new web projects.

This chapter will give you a look at other new properties you can use today as well as what is to come. In some cases, these features have much less support in current browsers than the features covered elsewhere. Included in this chapter is information on current browser support for each property to help you make an informed decision about which of these properties have wide enough support to find their way into your projects. Check the already mentioned browser support charts or When Can I Use... (*http://caniuse.com/*) for detailed and current browser support information before deciding whether to use each property.

The box-shadow Property

Drop shadows, either solid or with feathered edges, can be drawn behind content boxes using the box-shadow property. CSS3 box shadows are more flexible than what you might be able to do with older techniques such as using a fixed-sized, semitransparent PNG image as the background image of an item. The box-shadow property can take one or more comma-separated <shadow> definitions.

- none: No shadow is drawn.
- <shadow>: The definition of a shadow.

The description of a CSS <shadow> has three parts: two to four `<length>` values, a shadow `<color>`, and an optional `inset` keyword. The `<length>` values represent, in order, the horizontal offset of the shadow, the vertical offset of the shadow, the blur distance (`0` is no blur), and a spread distance (the growth or contraction of a shadow from the size of an element). The first two values, or the offsets, are required. If the blur or spread lengths are not supplied, they are assumed to be `0`.

Shown in **Figure 14.1**, the following code demonstrates a sharp box shadow (no blur radius) and a fuzzy shadow (with a blur radius set).

Figure 14.1
Example of a box shadow without and with a blur radius.

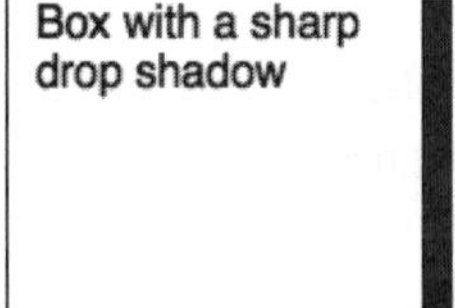


```
div.one {
    /* for Firefox */
    -moz-box-shadow: 10px 10px rgba(0,0,0,0.8);
    /* for Safari and Chrome */
    -webkit-box-shadow: 10px 10px rgba(0,0,0,0.8);
    /* W3C specs */
    box-shadow: 10px 10px rgba(0,0,0,0.8);
}
div.two {
    /* for Firefox */
    -moz-box-shadow: 10px 10px 20px rgba(0,0,0,0.8);
    /* for Safari and Chrome */
    -webkit-box-shadow: 10px 10px 20px rgba(0,0,0,0.8);
    /* W3C specs */
    box-shadow: 10px 10px 20px rgba(0,0,0,0.8);
}
```

(continues on next page)

```
[...]
<div class="one">
   Box with a sharp drop shadow
</div>
<div class="two">
   Box with a drop shadow with a large blur
</div>
```

Shadows can be draw inside an element using the `inset` keyword in the definition of a shadow. Replacing the inside shadow made with a background image used on the text input field in Figure 11.4 can be done with the following code (**Figure 14.2**):

```
div.one {
   /* for Firefox */
   -moz-box-shadow: inset 10px 10px rgba(0,0,0,0.8);
   /* for Safari and Chrome */
   -webkit-box-shadow: inset 10px 10px rgba(0,0,0,0.8);
   /* W3C specs */
   box-shadow: inset 10px 10px rgba(0,0,0,0.8);
}
div.two {
   /* for Firefox */
   -moz-box-shadow: inset 10px 10px 20px rgba(0,0,0,0.8);
   /* for Safari and Chrome */
   -webkit-box-shadow: inset 10px 10px 20px rgba(0,0,0,0.8);
   /* W3C specs */
   box-shadow: inset 10px 10px 20px rgba(0,0,0,0.8);
}
[...]
<div class="one">
   Box with a sharp inset shadow
</div>
```

```
<div class="two">
   Box with a inset shadow with a large blur
</div>
```

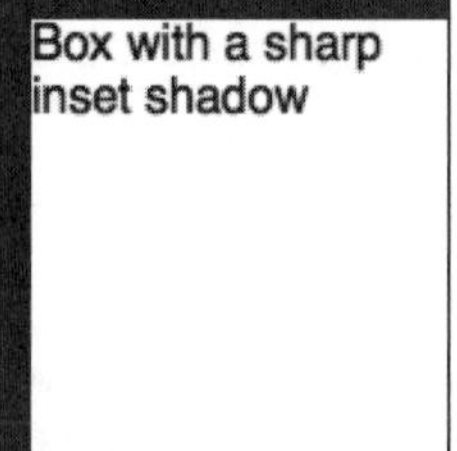

Figure 14.2 *Example of an inset box shadow without and with a blur radius.*

The `box-shadow` property is supported now in Firefox 3.5+, Safari 3.0+, Chrome 1+, Opera 10.5+, and Internet Explorer 9+. Safari 5+ and Chrome 4+ offer full support of the `box-shadow` definitions, but older versions don't support the `inset` keyword. See my blog post at *http://placenamehere.com/article/384/* for more information on creating a cross-browser drop shadow using both the `box-shadow` property and the proprietary IE filter extension to apply a similar shadow in IE6 through IE8.

The `background-size` Property

Through CSS 2.1, background images were displayed at their default/inherent size. If you wanted to have an image behind an element be the fill size of the element, you would either have to make sure the size of the image and the element matched or have to use some trickery to place the image in a `<div>` positioned and sized to the content element but with a lower `z-index` value.

But now images can be scaled or resized using the `background-size` property that accepts two values: the first for the horizontal sizing and the second for the vertical sizing (if one value is given, the second is assumed to be `auto`).

- auto: Scales the side of the image so that the inherent aspect ratio of the image is maintained; if both values are auto, the image appears at its normal size (default).
- <percentage>: Scales the size of the background image to a percentage of the element's (not image's) background area in the specified direction.
- <length>: Scales the side of the background image to the specified length.

Figure 14.3 demonstrates the background-size property when these <percentage> and <length> values are used for sizing.

```
div.one {
   background: url(images/background_sizing_tile.png)
➥ no-repeat top left;
}
div.two {
   background: url(images/background_sizing_tile.png)
➥ no-repeat top left;
   /* for Firefox 3.6 */
   -moz-background-size: 100% 50px;
   /* for Safari and Chrome */
   -webkit-background-size: 100% 50px;
   /* for Opera */
   -o-background-size: 100% 50px;
   /* W3C specs */
   background-size: 100% 50px;
}
div.three {
   background: url(images/background_sizing_tile.png)
➥ no-repeat top left;
```

```
    /* for Firefox 3.6 */
    -moz-background-size: 100% 100%;
    /* for Safari and Chrome */
    -webkit-background-size: 100% 100%;
    /* for Opera */
    -o-background-size: 100% 100%;
    /* W3C specs */
    background-size: 100% 100%;
}
[...]
<div class="one">
    Background with no background sizing
</div>
<div class="two">
    Background with background-size set to 100% 50px
</div>
<div class="three">
    Background with background-size set to 100% 100%
</div>
```

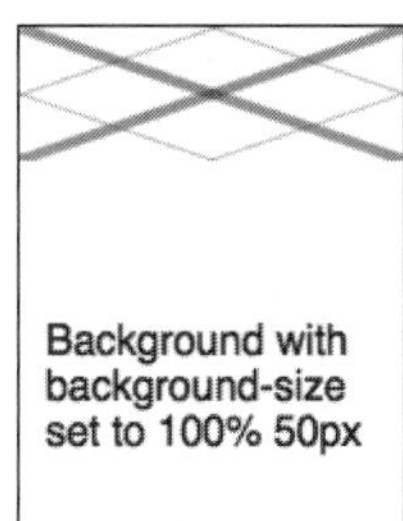

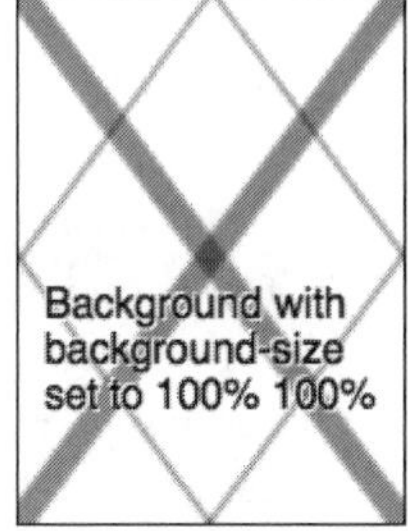

Figure 14.3 *Example of a background image without* background-size *set and with* background-size *set to specific dimensions.*

As an alternative to the paired values shown earlier, the singular keywords `contain` and `cover` describe explicit behaviors for how the background may fill the available space.

- `contain`: The background image is sized as large as it can be so that it is completely contained within the available space; if the aspect ratio of the image is different from the background area, then one side will be 100 percent, and another will be smaller than the available length.
- `cover`: The background image is sized so that it scales up (or down) to completely fill the background area; if the aspect ratio of the image is different from the background area, then one side will be 100 percent, and another will be larger than the available length and appear cropped.

Figure 14.4 displays the `background-size` property when set using these keywords.

```
div.one {
   background: url(images/background_sizing_tile.png)
➥no-repeat top left;
}
div.two {
   background: url(images/background_sizing_tile.png)
➥no-repeat top left;
   /* for Firefox */
   -moz-background-size: cover;
   /* for Safari and Chrome */
   -webkit-background-size: cover;
   /* for Opera */
   -o-background-size: cover;
   /* W3C specs */
   background-size: cover;
}
```

```
div.three {
   background: url(images/background_sizing_tile.png)
➥no-repeat top left;
   /* for Firefox */
   -moz-background-size: contain;
   /* for Safari and Chrome */
   -webkit-background-size: contain;
   /* for Opera */
   -o-background-size: contain;
   /* W3C specs */
   background-size: contain;
}
[...]
<div class="one">
   Background with no background sizing
</div>
<div class="two">
   Background with background-size set to cover
</div>
<div class="three">
   Background with background-size set to contain
</div>
```

Figure 14.4 *Examples of* `background-size` *keywords.*

Background image sizing is supported in some form by Firefox 3.6+, Safari 3+, Chrome 4+, Opera 9.5+, and IE9+.

Color Gradients

The background property is getting another enhancement with a feature that allows for the definition of a color <gradient> value to take the place of a more conventional file-based background-image.

Color gradients are lighter weight and more flexible than attempting to create the properly sized gradient via an image file in Photoshop or other graphic creation tool. Gradients can be linear or radial and can optionally transition between one or more color "stops."

The following code builds a linear gradient that shifts from solid black to solid white and then back to black (**Figure 14.5**):

```
div {
   [...]
   /* for unsupported browsers */
   background: #aaa;
   /* for Firefox */
   background: -moz-linear-gradient(top, #000, #fff, #000);
   /* for Safari and Chrome */
   background: -webkit-gradient(linear, left top, left
➥bottom, from(#000), to(#000), color-stop(0.5,#fff));
   /* W3C specs */
   background: linear-gradient(left top, #000, #fff, #000);
}
```

The direction (or angle) of the gradient can be controlled, as can the distance it takes to transition colors.

Figure 14.5
A linear gradient with three colors.

Unfortunately, the draft of the CSS3 Images Module specification and the syntax used by WebKit browsers and Firefox vary a good deal, so the definition of the gradient is currently quite complex. Westciv has a handy tool to create gradients and code for either browser at *http://westciv.com/tools/gradients/*.

CSS gradients are supported in their experimental forms in Firefox 3.6+, Safari 4+, and Chrome 3+.

Border Images

Flexible, image-based borders can replace the standard border styles using the `border-image` property. This is achieved by slicing the border area into a nine-segment grid representing each of the corners of the border area and the sides, as shown in **Figure 14.6**. A single image file is similarly split into nine segments and mapped to each of the areas of the border area and the center of the container.

Figure 14.6
An example of the nine-quadrants of an image used for a border background.

The value for `border-image` property is comprised of an image reference, a description where the image is divided to create nine segments, how those segments are positioned, and finally a description of how they tile to fill the available area.

border-image-source

The `border-image-source` property accepts a reference to the image used as the border image.

border-image-slice

`border-image-slice` defines where the four lines that slice an image into segments are positioned, inset from each of the four sides of the image. For the image displayed in Figure 14.6, it would make sense to position these dividing lines 30 pixels from each edge to create nine even segments. The distance from each edge can be measured by the following values:

- <number>: The number of pixels (or the coordinates for SVG images). Pixel units are implied for bitmap background images, and the unit should be left off.
- <percentage>: A percentage value based on the dimensions of the image.

A width for the border can optionally be assigned via the `border-image-slice` property by adding a forward slash (/) after the slice position values. These width measurements are the same as the `border-width` property, and if both properties are set, then the border width values set as part of `border-image-slice` override those set in the `border-width` property. The following example sets the slices that segment the image to be 30 units from each edge, with a border width of 30 pixel for the top and bottom border and 15 pixel for the left and right.

```
div.one {
    /* for Firefox */
    -moz-border-image-slice: 30 / 30px 15px;
    /* for Safari and Chrome */
    -webkit-border-image-slice: 30 / 30px 15px;
    /* W3C specs */
    border-image-slice: 30 / 30px 15px;
}
```

tip **The border width behavior of `border-image-slice` allows you to set one width for browsers that only understand the traditional border properties and alter the size for those that understand `border-image`.**

border-image-repeat

The `border-image-repeat` property defines how the slices of the border image fill the flexible space on the side borders and middle portion of the border area. You can use one or two of the following keywords:

- `stretch`: The image slice is scaled to fit the available space, without repeating (default).
- `repeat`: The image slice is not scaled but tiled to fill the available space. As a result, the image may appear cropped on some edges.
- `round`: The image slice is tiled; however, only whole images are used. The tiles are then scaled evenly to fill the remaining space.

If only one keyword is provided, it is applied to both the borders and the center section.

border-image *(Shorthand)*

The shorthand `border-image` accepts the previous three subproperties, as well as the additional properties of `border-image-width` and border-image-outside (that describe where the images are drawn in the border area) in the order <border-image-source>, <border-image-slice>, <border-image-repeat>.

Figure 14.7 uses the image from Figure 14.6 as a border image and demonstrates the difference between border-image-repeat values.

```
div {
   /* set common width for all browsers */
   border-width: 30px;
}
div.one {
   /* for Firefox */
   -moz-border-image: url(images/border_background_tile.png)
➥30 30 30 30 round round;
   /* for Safari and Chrome */
   -webkit-border-image: url(images/border_background_tile.png)
➥30 30 30 30 round round;
   /* W3C specs */
   border-image: url(images/border_background_tile.png) 30 30
➥30 30 round round;
}
div.two {
   /* for Firefox */
   -moz-border-image: url(images/border_background_tile.png)
➥30 30 30 30 stretch stretch;
   /* for Safari and Chrome */
   -webkit-border-image: url(images/border_background_tile.png)
➥30 30 30 30 stretch stretch;
   /* W3C specs */
   border-image: url(images/border_background_tile.png) 30 30
➥30 30 stretch stretch;
```

```
}
[...]
<div class="one">
   border image with sides and middle set to round
</div>
<div class="two">
   border image with sides and middle set to stretch
</div>
```

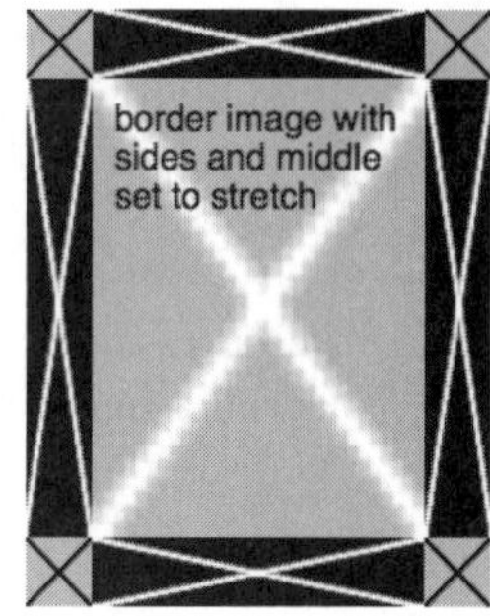

Figure 14.7 *Examples of border backgrounds with* `round` *and* `stretch` *values for* `border-image-repeat`.

Border backgrounds are supported in Firefox 3.5+, Opera 10.5+, Chrome 3+, and Safari 3.2+.

WAI-ARIA Roles

Though not explicitly CSS related, the Accessible Rich Internet Application (WAI-ARIA) specification (*http://www.w3.org/TR/wai-aria/*) provides definitions of common semantics of application widgets and states as a semantic layer to be added to existing HTML markup using the `role` attribute. Role types include `navigation`, `progressbar`, `alertdialog`, `tab`, and `tooltip`. By applying these roles to HTML elements, screen readers and other assistive devices can react to these items more appropriately than they would an element with a `class` or `id` of `progressbar`.

The CSS attribute selector can also leverage these role definitions, along with state-based attributes such as `aria-checked`, as hooks for styling, rather than relying on class attributes.

You can find more about WAI-ARIA roles and their usage in the spec on the W3C site (*http://www.w3.org/TR/wai-aria/usage*).

The `calc()` Function

The `calc()` function lets you replace any `<length>` value assignment with a mathematical expression rather than a fixed-length unit. These arithmetic expressions can be built with the operators +, -, *, /, `min`, `max`, and `mod`.

The problem of leftover pixels that arose in Chapter 7 when mixing percentage values and fixed lengths (Figure 7.9) can be solved by using `calc()` instead. **Figure 14.8** shows the updated multicolumn, flexible layout.

```
/* modifications to 7.9 using calc() */
.main_left,
.main_center {
   /* for unsupported browsers */
   width: 48%;
   /* for Firefox 4 */
   width: -moz-calc(50% - 7px);
   /* W3C specs */
   width: calc(50% - 7px);
}
```

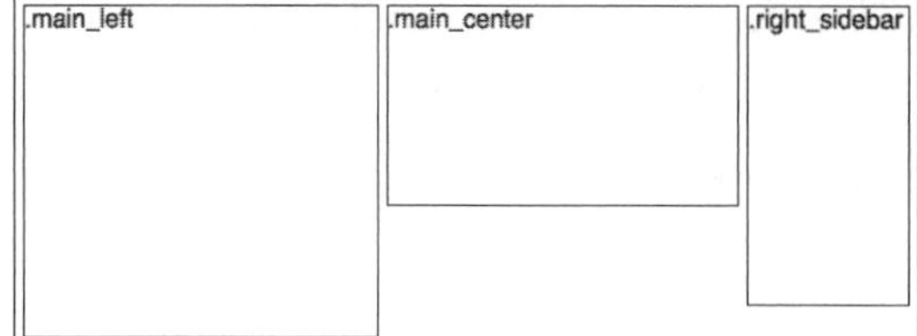

Figure 14.8 *A flexible, multicolumn layout using* `calc()`.

In the previous code, the available width of the container is split shared by the margins between the boxes (the four vertical side borders), with the remaining area split evenly between the two flexible columns. The arithmetic you would use to calculate what is left over after the fixed area is 100% – 10px – 4px. That area split between each column and cleaned up a bit is 100%/2 – 14px/2.

`calc()` will be supported in upcoming browsers including Internet Explorer 9 and Firefox 4.

Transformations and Rotations

Using CSS transforms, you can rotate, skew, or scale elements.

Transforming an element does not change the flow of a document; instead, the element takes up its pretransformed shape in the document much in the same way that relative positioned elements behave.

transform

The `transform` property is used to define one or more `<transform-functions>` for the specified element.

- none: No transform is applied.
- `<transform-function>`: The description of a transform to be applied to an element.

Values for **<transform-function>**

The following are values for `<transform-function>`:

- `translateX(<length>)`: Translates the element by the specified amount on the x-axis.
- `translateY(<length>)`: Translates the element by the specified amount on the y-axis.
- `translate(<length>[, <length>])`: Translates the element by the specified amount; the first value is along the x-axis, and the second is along the y-axis (0 if not specified).
- `scaleX(<number>)`: Scales the element by the specified factor along the x-axis.
- `scaleY(<number>)`: Scales the element by the specified factor along the x-axis.
- `scale(<number>[, <number>])`: Scales the element by the specified factor along each axis; the first value is the x-axis, and the second is along the y-axis (equal to x if not specified).
- `rotate(<angle>)`: Rotates an element around the origin by the specified angle (in deg units); a positive angle rotates the element in a clockwise direction.
- `skewX(<angle>)`: Skews the element along the x-axis by the specified angle (in deg units).
- `skewY(<angle>)`: Skews the element along the y-axis by the specified angle (in deg units).
- `skew(<angle>[, <angle>])`: Skews the element along each axis by the specified angle (in deg units); the first value is the x-axis, and the second is along the y-axis (0 if not specified).

- matrix(<number>, <number>, <number>, <number>, <number>, <number>): Specifies a linear transformation matrix (*http://en.wikipedia.org/wiki/Linear_transformation#Examples_of_linear_transformation_matrices*) for transformation of the element.

Starting with the dated flag graphic used the negative positioning demonstration in Figure 7.6, you can rotate the flag and text by 270 degrees to sit alongside of the content item it is matched with.

```
/* modifications to 7.6 using transform */
article time {
   /* adjust positioning */
   top: 29px;
   left: -81px;

   /* for Firefox */
   -moz-transform: rotate(270deg);
   /* for Safari and Chrome */
   -webkit-transform: rotate(270deg);
   /* for Opera */
   -o-transform: rotate(270deg);
   /* W3C specs */
   transform: rotate(270deg);
}
```

In the previous code example, the element was rotated and then positioned with absolute positioning to properly place it (**Figure 14.9** on the next page). The position before the rotation (and thus in any browser that doesn't support transitions) is shown by the dotted outline.

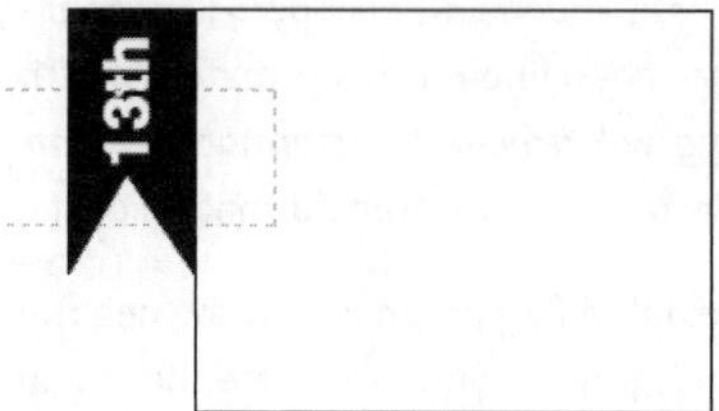

Figure 14.9
The flag and text content is rotated by 270 degrees to a vertical position.

If this position before the translation is undesirable (for example, because it is shifted too low), it may be better to position the element as it was in the original example and then apply two transforms to get it to its final appearance: rotation and translation (**Figure 14.10**).

```
/* modifications to 7.6 using two transforms */
article time {
   /* for Firefox */
   -moz-transform: rotate(270deg) translate(-19px,-31px);
   /* for Safari and Chrome */
   -webkit-transform: rotate(270deg) translate(-19px,-31px);
   /* for Opera */
   -o-transform: rotate(270deg) translate(-19px,-31px);
   /* W3C specs */
   transform: rotate(270deg) translate(-19px,-31px);
}
```

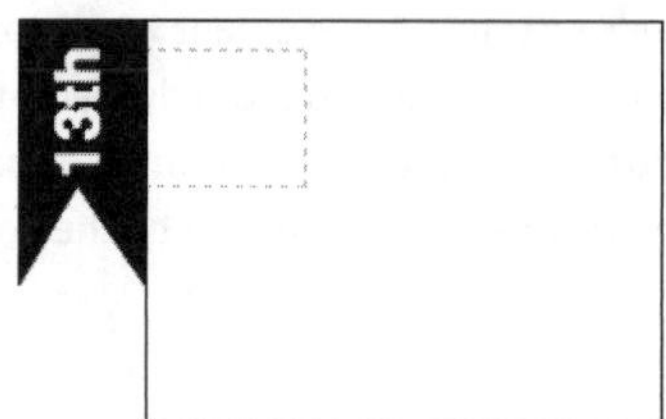

Figure 14.10
The flag and text content is rotated and translated, leaving a more desirable nontransformed state.

transform-origin

The origin for any transform is by default the center of the element (50% 50%). You can adjust this origin using the `transform-origin` property, allowing for rotation around a different point. `transform-origin` accepts two values: the first is the horizontal position of the element, and the second is the vertical position. Fixed units such as px units, negative values, and values greater than 100 percent are all accepted, allowing for the point of origin to be moved outside the element. Also accepted are keywords for defining the origin point, including `left`, `center`, and `right` along the x-axis and `top`, `center`, and `bottom` along the y-axis.

Figure 14.11 shows how the effects of a rotation of an element change when the transform-origin is changed from its default position.

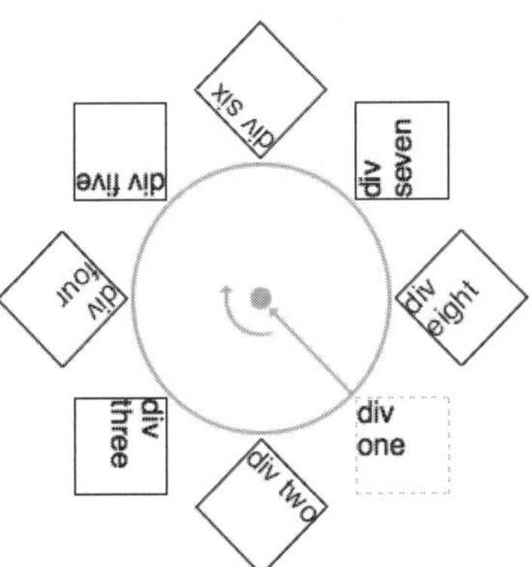

Figure 14.11 *Elements rotated around a transform origin. The diagonal arrow represents the new position of the origin; the circle represents the rotational transform.*

note **For the sake of brevity, only the code targeting Firefox is displayed in the following code.**

```
div {
   height: 50px;
   width: 50px;
```

(continues on next page)

```
    border: 1px solid #000;
    -moz-transform-origin: -100% -100%;
}
div.one {
    border: 1px dashed #ccc;
}
div.two {
    -moz-transform: rotate(45deg);
}
div.three {
    -moz-transform: rotate(90deg);
}
div.four {
    -moz-transform: rotate(135deg);
}
div.five {
    -moz-transform: rotate(180deg);
}
div.six {
    -moz-transform: rotate(225deg);
}
div.seven {
    -moz-transform: rotate(270deg);
}
div.eight {
    -moz-transform: rotate(315deg);
}
[...]
<div class="one">div one</div>
<div class="two">div two</div>
<div class="three">div three</div>
```

```
<div class="four">div four</div>
<div class="five">div five</div>
<div class="six">div six</div>
<div class="seven">div seven</div>
<div class="eight">div eight</div>
```

The second value is optional. In cases where it is left off, it is assumed to be `center`.

The CSS3 `transform` property, its values, and the `transform-origin` property are supported in some form by Safari 3.2+, Chrome 3+, Opera 10.5+, Firefox 3.5+, and Internet Explorer 9+.

Transitions

CSS transitions are a way to define parameters for animating changes to CSS properties on a specified element. Changes to styles can occur because of updates in element state (`:hover`, `:valid`, and so on), scripted changes to styles on an element, or other scripted changes to the DOM structure causing a change in how selectors are applied.

transition-property

`transition-property` designates which CSS property or properties are animated when a change occurs. Animations can occur with most CSS properties; however, some properties such as `background-image` and `text-decoration` cannot.

- none: No properties will be animated (default).
- `all`: All properties that can be animated will be.
- `<property-name>[, <property-name>]`: A comma-separated list of one or more properties that can be animated if a change occurs.

`transition-duration`

The time it takes to transition from the original value of a property to the final value can be set via the `transition-duration` property.

- `<time>`: The time it takes for a transition to complete; in seconds (s units)

`transition-timing-function`

By default the transition between values of a property is animated along an even, linear function. You can alter this change via the `transition-timing-function` by choosing between several built-in functions or a custom cubic-Bezier curve.

- `ease` | `linear` | `ease-in` | `ease-out` | `ease-in-out`: Keywords representing different types of built-in functions for animation
- `cubic-bezier(<number>, <number>, <number>, <number>)`: A transition function to define a custom cubic-Bezier curve

`transition-delay`

You can add a delay before a transition using the `translation-delay` property.

- `<time>`: The time it takes before for a transition begins animating; in seconds (s units)

`transition` *(Shorthand)*

The shorthand `transition` property accepts one or more groups of transition subproperty groups in the order: `<transition-property>` `<transition-duration>` `<transition-timing-function>` `<transition-delay>`. The following code example defines the transform for the hover state on an image and applies a basic easing animation to the transition.

```
img {
   /* for Firefox 4 */
   -moz-transition: -moz-transform 0.5s ease-out;
   /* for Safari and Chrome */
   -webkit-transition: -webkit-transform 0.5s ease-out;
   /* For Opera */
   -o-transition: -o-transform 0.5s ease-out;
   /* W3C specification */
   transition: transform 0.5s ease-out;
}
img:hover {
   /* for Firefox 4 */
   -moz-transform: scale(1.5, 1.5);
   /* for Safari and Chrome */
   -webkit-transform: scale(1.5, 1.5);
   /* For Opera */
   -o-transform: scale(1.5, 1.5);
   /* W3C specification */
   transform: scale(1.5, 1.5);
}
[...]
<img src="images/hover_me.png" width="90" height="90"
➥ alt="Hover Me" />
```

The Mozilla Developer Center has a thorough article on working with transitions at *https://developer.mozilla.org/en/CSS/CSS_transitions*.

CSS transitions are supported in Safari 3.2+ Chrome 3+, Opera 10.5+, Firefox 4+, and Internet Explorer 9+.

Index

SYMBOLS AND NUMBERS

A

B

C

D

E

H

I

J

K

L

M

T

U

V

W

X

Y

Z